973.9
ODON. W9-BFA-096

AMERICA'S
Man on Horseback

❧

A Fable?

Also by Guy Odom

Mothers, Leadership, and Success

AMERICA'S
Man on Horseback

A Fable?

GUY ODOM

Beaufort Books Publishers
New York

This book is printed on acid-free paper, and its binding materials have been chosen for strength and durability.

Library of Congress Cataloging-in-Publication Data
Odom, Guy R., 1931–
America's man on horseback : a fable? / by Guy R. Odom.
p.   cm.
Includes bibliographical references and index.
ISBN 0-8253-0501-2 (hardcover : alk. paper)
1. United States — Politics and government — 1993–   2. United States — Economic Policy — 1993–   3. United States — Social policy — 1993–   I. Title.
JK271.026   1998
973.929 — dc21   97-44904
                                                                        CIP

man on horseback, a military figure who presents himself as the savior of the country during a period of crisis and either assumes or threatens to assume dictatorial powers.

The Random House Dictionary of the English Language

Contents

Tables

Acknowledgments

To all the wonderful people who contributed suggestions, advice, and encouragement — thank you. I am grateful for your help during the development of *America's Man on Horseback*.

Your names remain unrecorded since I respect your concern that satire is most often misconstrued and that arsenic is more digestible than truth. Still, you know who you are and will recognize your thoughts and contributions throughout this book.

Also, many thanks to those who inadvertently inspired *America's Man on Horseback* — you, too, know who you are.

Guy Odom

AMERICA'S
Man on Horseback

❦

A Fable?

Introduction

✿

Earthquakes are predictable, their causes provable. Successful societies are similar — their demises are equally predictable, but the causes are only partially identifiable. And like an earthquake, a society's demise can be dated . . . but only with hindsight. Few scientists, if any, would attempt to predict a major earthquake, its location, and its occurrence within fifteen years, since no one would believe them. The same fate awaits Cassandras who foresee catastrophic political and social changes fifteen years hence. So it is with me. Only time will determine whether *America's Man on Horseback* is overstatement or understatement, fable or prophecy, cynicism or truth, demagoguery or enlightenment, horror or humor — satire or reality.

In 1846, James Polk was the eleventh U.S. president, Iowa became the twenty-ninth state in the Union, and war broke out between the United States and Mexico. Few Americans that year anticipated an American civil war fifteen years later, in 1861.

In 1926, Calvin Coolidge was the thirtieth president, U.S. Marines landed in Nicaragua to put down insurrection, and Colonel William "Billy" Mitchell, suspended from rank and duty for five years, resigned from the army. During that year of the Roaring Twenties, how many Americans dreamed that the United States would soon enter another world war? Billy Mitchell did.

1

During World War I, Mitchell was the outstanding combat air commander; he was highly decorated by the U.S. and foreign governments and was promoted to brigadier general in 1918. After World War I, as a peacetime colonel and assistant chief of the air service, he advocated a separate U.S. air force and greater preparedness for an inevitable, and imminent, second world war. Colonel Mitchell was court-martialed and convicted of insubordination in 1925 for privately and publicly voicing his unpopular views to a war-weary nation — a severe penalty, indeed, for envisioning World War II early. (And in 1926, only a few astute investors made themselves ready for the stock market crash three years later.)

In 1950, President Harry Truman held office, the United States recognized the new state of Vietnam and sent advisers there to teach the use of weapons to the Vietnamese, and American forces under General Douglas MacArthur were committed to the war in Korea. Americans that year had no idea that in just fifteen years the nation would enter into hostilities with North Vietnam that would end in defeat.

Today, President William Clinton sits in the Oval Office, inflation is "under control," and the stock market regularly sets new highs. (In spite of this, more than a few sophisticated investors, particularly older ones, realize that no stock market rises forever.) Tectonic stress continues to build along the San Andreas Fault, little different from the escalating social tensions that have been building in the nation for a generation and a half. In time both will erupt. And in fifteen years, the *political* reverberations may be more violent than any earthquake in California.

In *America's Man on Horseback,* I anticipate that conditions will worsen ten times by 2013. Instead of one-at-a-time race riots in Los Angeles, New York, or the District of Columbia, sack-and-burn racial anarchy will explode in ten major cities simultaneously. There will be ten times as many corrupt politicians holding office and ten times as many financial scams. Inflation will increase tenfold. Gang warfare, illegal drug use, murder, rape, robbery, and terrorism will be ten times as bad.

Of course this grim scenario contradicts the majesty of 1998 America, with its modern communications, resplendent technology, conspicuous wealth, and the "safety" of mutual fund investments, which most Americans believe make "today" so much different and better than "yesterday." So who but a fool could make a comparison between this magnificent achievement and other great, but failed, societies? Perhaps too many pay attention to the obscure and too few to the obvious. One during my time went so far as to say that "he [who looks to history] makes the mistake of extending the same trend into the future that has gone on in the past, failing to recognize the many moderating influences that a society and its many parts provide in such a situation." Or, as Henry Ford scoffed, "History is more or less bunk," confirming this deep, unshakable belief that the United States is immune from the lessons of history.

So while a dictator is a historically sound proposition, and while this single premise of "ten times worse than today" makes the idea of a "man on horseback" to rein in an out-of-control nation plausible, and perhaps even attractive, it will be a difficult "first" for this nation and its citizens.

Should social conditions deteriorate that dramatically, what actions would you expect the then president to take to "clean up the mess"? How should he deal with crime and punishment, corrupt politicians, crooked lawyers, dishonest investment bankers, gangs, race riots, and domestic and foreign terrorism? What about inflation, immigration problems, and the abandonment of the American work ethic?

What advice would *you* give the "man on horseback"? Would you couch your counsel in politically correct terms? Even speaking to a dictator? Perhaps you would speak more bluntly if you or a family member had been the victim of a burglary, robbery, financial scam, or corporate high-handedness. Others might speak with outright anger — relatives or friends of homicide victims, particularly parents of murdered children; family members whose loved ones were maimed or killed by drunk drivers; parents of hemophiliac children infected with AIDS through blood transfusions; women who were raped. And how would members of our armed forces, particularly marines, respond?

Should, in time, a dictator assume power and reign over America, people will certainly then ask, "Why weren't we warned?"

History tells us that warnings are not only naive but wasteful.

Just as the Greeks of the Hellenistic period ignored Polybius, contemporary Americans are equally inattentive, for, as Alexis de Tocqueville made clear, "It is very difficult to make the inhabitants of democracies listen when one is not talking about themselves. They do not hear what is said to them because they are always very preoccupied with what they are doing. . . . Whenever conditions are equal, public opinion brings immense weight to bear on every individual. It surrounds, directs, and oppresses him." But over time, and without fail, public opinion does change.

America's Man on Horseback offers no suggestions for correcting the social ills of contemporary society. Will it serve as a "wake-up call"? Possibly, but doubtful, since many of those asleep believe that they are only "resting their eyes." As with previous successful civilizations at their crest, it appears that the agents of America's decline are too entrenched to be reversed. Nevertheless, I wish to provoke anger in the reader, to evoke strong personal emotion, heighten individual awareness — whether the anger is directed at politicians, as I suggest, or at me. (When Jonathan Swift, the greatest satirist in the English language, published his essay *A Modest Proposal* in aid of Ireland, he became the most reviled person in Europe. Few recognized his satire; Swift himself became the target.)

It will not be easy to find a reader who values the whole of *America's Man on Horseback*. Still, there will be individuals who recognize and appreciate parts of it. Moreover, as national circumstances and public opinion continue to change, the book may spark new interest and discussion, one chapter at a time. It may awaken in many Americans dormant thoughts of unease brought about by the decadence and corruption narcotizing our nation. It may offer a catharsis to those Americans harmed by current conditions. And it may even provide the thoughtful and receptive with insights on how to protect themselves and their families from vicissitudes created by conditions ten times worse than those faced today.

One cited purpose of Machiavelli's when he wrote his "little book" *The Prince* was to secure employment. This is not the case with me; I work for myself and my needs are more modest. Nor do I fear a military court martial such as Colonel Mitchell faced; it has been many years since I served in the U.S. Navy. Does *America's*

Man on Horseback represent my wishes for the future of this great nation? Certainly not! American democracy has allowed me to fare better than my greatest childhood ambitions.

When America's "man on horseback" prevails, he may find interesting what I attribute as the cause of our nation's decline. The "man" may even consider humorous my views of contemporary America. Beyond this — other than the premise that an American dictator will emerge between 2013 and 2029 — all that you read is writer's fancy. I tiptoe here and there, but I lack the courage to describe the real "man on horseback." If I were to depict his true draconian potential, it would be ten times worse than any I outline in this book . . . and no one would believe me.

CHAPTER ONE

Greetings and Salutations

❧

The time will arrive when decadence and lawlessness
become so pervasive that even angels are burned by
corruption. Then comes America's Man on Horseback.

GUY ODOM

Welcome, Mr. President. America has watched and waited ten generations for your arrival!

I know not the final episode that delivered the presidency of the United States of America to you. Whether you were elected as president or were the vice president when the president abdicated, committed suicide, or was assassinated; or whether you became president by another path — this matters not. Your presidency emanated from the electoral process.

With the histories of failed civilizations on my side, I expect your inauguration to take place around the year 2013. It is doubtful, though possible, that you will arrive earlier, but surely no later than 2029. Chaotic conditions make it so.

Your defenders laugh and tell funny stories while the opposition cries foul. As you savor your inauguration, your enemies denounce you as America's first dictator. Your supporters celebrate and proclaim you the deliverer and the emancipator. Some of your more revenge-minded followers hail you as the prosecutor.

But you are above politics. You are America's Man on Horseback. You act, not merely talk.

DURING the middle years of the country's first 250-year cycle, sages feared your advent, expecting an oppressor or a tyrant. Perhaps the first American-to-be to anticipate you was an illegitimate sixteen-year-old counting clerk in a West Indies trading company in 1771. At that time he wrote, "A Prime Minister, like a Commander in Chief . . . I think this wise regulation a wholesome restraint on the people, whose turbulence at times . . . requires a Dictator." Alexander Hamilton went on to become the most important aide-de-camp to General George Washington during the Revolutionary War — the Age of Outburst of the American Republic — and later he became one of the principal authors of the United States Constitution. Hamilton was the strongest advocate of the provisions that created the office of the president in which the powers of commander in chief of the armed forces are vested.

George Washington, a "man on horseback," was our country's first liberator. Since 1964, after the nation's ninth generation emerged and the Age of Decadence began, the longing of U.S. citizens for the accession of the second liberator became more compelling as turbulence increased and the cry for order became more strident.

It is inevitable that you became president at this fated time in our nation's history. The limited options available left Americans little choice but you. Your ascendancy begins as America's Age of Decadence ends — a time when the country is not worth dying for; when the dishonest prosper and the honest suffer; when fainthearted politicians jabber, babble, and stall while criminals steal, rape, and murder with impunity. Frivolity and license prevail. The people turn to you because security and safety have become more important than freedom. You rise to power because history repeats itself. Niccolo Machiavelli anticipated 1998 America when he wrote:

> . . . all the past evils and all the other disorders that appear in it. First, there is neither union nor friendship, except among those who have knowingly committed some wickedness either against their fatherland or against private persons. And because religion and fear of God have been eliminated in all, an oath and faith given last only as long as they are useful; so men make use of them not to observe them but to serve as a means of being able

to deceive more easily. And the more easily and surely the deception succeeds, the more glory and praise is acquired from it; by this, harmful men are praised as industrious and good men are blamed as fools. And truly, all that can be corrupted and that can corrupt others is thrown together; the young are lazy, the old lascivious; both sexes at every age are full of foul customs, for which good laws, because they are spoiled by wicked use, are no remedy.

You have promised to deliver the honest, hardworking, law-abiding minority from their persecution by the ungodly and the unconscionable, who constitute a near-majority of Americans at your ascendancy. You will stop the criminal terrorism of Americans, not simply mouth platitudes such as "build more prisons" or "prevent crime." No longer will America's public schools be used as holding pens while futilely attempting to teach children to "just say no" to drugs, stealing, and killing. No longer will truces be negotiated among the leaders of America's ethnic slaughter. Your vow to stop crime pits you against millions of dishonest Americans.

Because of your reputation for action, even unscrupulous Americans, in fear of violent criminals, support you rather than your opponents. Dishonest Americans — welfare defrauders, income tax cheats, corporate destroyers of the environment, and others — will suffer even the devil if they believe he will keep them in the land of the living.

You have become president partially because of your aspirations but mainly because the bad — out of avarice and ambition — and the good — out of necessity — participated in ruining America. As George Washington freed America from 6.7 million Britishers, you have promised to free the nation from the clutches of five times that number of criminals and politicians. You have vowed to liberate Americans from the destroyers of freedom.

You are the first president empowered to rid the country of crime and punish all criminals, whether violent or nonviolent, who rob Americans of their lives, their safety, and their livelihoods. Even Thomas Jefferson foresaw radical changes:

Prudence, indeed, will dictate that Governments long established should not be changed for light and transient Causes; and
accordingly all Experience hath shown, that Mankind are more
disposed to suffer, while Evils are sufferable, than to right themselves by abolishing the Forms to which they are accustomed.
But when a long Train of Abuses and Usurpations, pursuing invariably the same Object, evidences a design to reduce them
under absolute Despotism, it is their right, it is their duty, to
throw off such Government, and to provide new Guards for
their future Security.

Mr. President, you are the new guard for American security.
And you will succeed. Mao Tse-tung confronted two and a half
times more millions than you; he succeeded. But avoid the excesses of an older Mao Tse-tung who, after revolutionary fervor diminished, murdered millions to retain precarious control of his
faltering regime.

While different from Mao's, your task is equally enormous. As
the nation simultaneously ends one ten-generation cycle and
begins another, you will be the one to bury the shed skin of the
despairing and decadent Republic and midwife the birth of an
Empire.

You, America's Man on Horseback, will make whole again a
fragmented America that has lost its way. Only you can restore our
one language, one broad-based culture, one common identity.
Since it is impossible to legislate morality, your virtuous undertak-
ings will serve as an example and remind all of their obligations. I
trust that you

- Are God-fearing
- Value righteousness
- Cherish justice
- Are calm and serene
- Do not vacillate
- Do not experience fear
- Cherish the principle of self-control
- Have neither narrow predilections nor obstinate antipathies

- Do not seek personal revenge
- Give advance warning of unpleasant actions to come
- Benefit the population on the whole with your necessary cruelties
- Confer proper rewards on deserving men
- Are dignified but not proud
- Are firm and resolute and slow of speech

Granted, these values are utopian, and you have great needs for power and control. You are what you are, and you are in control. Become neither loved nor feared by all Americans. Love is an emotion that can be withdrawn, and fear crystallizes into hate. You must gain first the respect of America's good people and later their trust; it is a greater tribute to be trusted than to be loved. You will earn the respect of honest, hard-working Americans by freeing them from government bureaucracy, high taxation, and oppression. The respect of the indolent will come, begrudgingly, over time, as a matter of course. And you will gain the respect of criminals only through cruelty, as they respect only what they fear; that criminals will hate you is inconsequential.

As you orchestrate America's transition from a dying Republic to a dynamic Empire, I offer knowledge of people and situations. I do not offer advice. Wise leaders do well to avoid unsolicited advice. Counselors think first of their own personal interests; only by accident do they consider your interests when offering unsolicited advice. It is different, however, when you ask for their ideas about specific situations. Your advisers should know that you accept nothing but the truth when you seek knowledge; then they will be honored that you desire their opinions. As you validate the worth of their ideas with action, you will bring out the best in your cohorts. But be careful to divorce yourself from flatterers and fools alike. Their conversations can lead at best to wasting your time, at worst to wasting your head.

I cannot be a member of your cabinet; I am not even a member of your time. If I am still in the land of the living at your presidency, I will be aged and have nothing of additional value to offer you. I will never respond with "I told you so," as I am only ink on paper; and I cannot betray a confidence nor reveal a confidential conversation. But I can help you as no other can as you pursue your goals.

The differences among my time, your time, and earlier times mean nothing. An overlooked idea of Plato can become an idea of yours. Your thoughts can travel along the same path as did the thoughts of Marcus Aurelius. I offer my services to glean history's granary of knowledge and bring you clean kernels of truth.

I endeavor to express my thoughts purely and concisely; I write in a simple and direct manner. I wish only to awaken in you the ideas that now lie dormant in your mind. I also want to offer caution against using those base beliefs that destroyed important leaders before you. At your leisure, turn a page for counsel; close the book when you tire.

Why do I offer this help? Altruism has little appeal to me. Just as you determine the worth of my words by acting on that about which I write, so too will you decide if I truly have lent you a hand. If so, I then will make a modest request of you.

SINCE 1976, I have anticipated your arrival. In the two centuries since Alexander Hamilton, others have as well, but I am the first to recognize you, to write to you, to wish you well. You are destined to redeem the United States, to reinstate the values of America of yore, and to protect this wonderful country from its enemies inside and outside its borders. I hail America's Man on Horseback.

Though it is 1998 as I write, I see you clearly, and I know you well, and I address you at the time of your presidency. I can describe you closely, though not with absolute certainty. You are around forty-five years of age. You served in the military. You exhibit a no-nonsense demeanor. You are not and never have been a fashion figure. People picture you no differently from how the contemporaries of Charlemagne, Genghis Khan, George Washington, Napoleon, Hitler, Churchill, or Stalin pictured them.

Your mother did not sleep with poisonous snakes nor have your father assassinated, as did Alexander's mother, Olympia. She did not terrify you with stories of demons while she beat you for breaking her rules, as did Luther's mother. Your demanding mother insisted that you excel — from infancy on — at everything she had you attempt. Possibly she became your friend, as did Napoleon's mother. Your mother inflicted corporal punishment when you crossed her or thwarted her demands. At the same time she likely enveloped you with praise for early childhood accomplishments. Your dominant mother knew even before your birth that you were destiny's golden child. And you have not failed her.

My conjecture about your past is not of importance to either of us, however. Your future task absorbs your mind and spirit; I speak to that purpose.

Who am I? View me as the child in the fable of the emperor's new clothes. I have the liberty to say exactly what I think because it is inconceivable that I could ever be a threat to you. I bring to your table (1) a superior knowledge of human behavior so as to explain history and predict future human affairs; (2) the ability to draw a pragmatic picture of the foibles of human behavior in my time; (3) the fruits of my research and studies and the predictability of the outcome of the tenth generation of splendid but failed civilizations; and (4) the guidance to help ensure that your historical reputation does not limit you to becoming a seventy-five-year man, as was Lenin, nor a 500-year man, as was Napoleon, nor even a 1000-year man, as was Julius Caesar. Neither should you be only a 2000-year man, as were Alexander and Charlemagne. Your impact on the world will be a thousand times greater than one of those seismic jolts that comes no more than once a millennium. It is important that God not weary of you early, as he did of Alexander, Caesar, and Napoleon.

Indeed, your ascendancy gives birth to a mighty transformation. But recognize that even those who champion change have secret doubts. It is only after repeated successes, as Machiavelli observed, that "men will be more ready to pursue a thing in motion than to move it." You will need a full thirty years to fulfill your destiny. Human nature has not deviated during the five centuries since Machiavelli wrote that "it has always been easier to maintain a power that by length of time has eliminated envy than to raise up a new one that for many causes could easily be eliminated." Your expanding reputation and initial successes will draw many to you; only the foolish will resist you. Remember also that human nature sympathizes with failure and resents success.

When confronting a problem, it is best to position yourself to choose the most advantageous of positive options. Failing that, it is still appealing to decide between a positive and a negative choice. The worst possible situation is where all options are negative — having to cull rather than being able to select, having to decide on a perilous course rather than facing certain danger. I can help you to foresee and thus avoid such situations.

Of course, the surest way to prevent failures is never to take chances. Yet inaction guarantees failure, and you are here because you are a risk taker. I offer nothing to diminish the risks; rather, I entreat you to take greater risks, and take them earlier. Fortune will reward you commensurately.

Y O U R willingness to take risks and to inflict pain, without regret or sorrow, yet with restraint, will place you on the crest of the first wave when America's tide turns. Move swiftly to secure and then expand your power. First, address crime and lawlessness throughout our nation; then, act to end ongoing domestic crises and remedy chronic problems. Next, establish discipline and new codes of conduct in order to sever the grip of decadence and make the new empire strong. In time you will be the sole arbiter of American good and evil.

Farther down the road your successes will herald a period of peace and quiet for our nation. But tranquility for America means travail for you. Domestic enemies, long submerged, will use such periods of calm to surface and attempt to undo you. Inevitably, terror as an agency to maintain control will move through your mind — from temptation to contemplation to implementation. Do not deceive yourself into thinking that you can maintain control for thirty years without utilizing this tool of terror.

At some future time you will preside over America's rebirth. With your leadership, our country stands to achieve a never-before-imagined greatness. May I serve you?

CHAPTER TWO

America's Ascent and Decline

❧

Perhaps now is the time to hark back to the period when America's social fabric began to unravel. Understanding better how we reached these depths may give you a truer grasp of the forces that brought you to your preeminence. In its decline, the United States has repeated the ten-generation, 250-year cycle of earlier great civilizations, a sequence described by Machiavelli:

> . . . usually provinces go most of the time, in the changes they make, from order to disorder and then pass again from disorder to order, for worldly things are not allowed by nature to stand still. As soon as they reach their ultimate perfection, having no further to rise, they must descend, and similarly, once they have descended and through their disorders arrived at the ultimate depth, since they cannot descend further, of necessity they must rise. Thus they are always descending from good to bad and rising from bad to good. For virtue gives birth to quiet, quiet to leisure, leisure to disorder, disorder to ruin; and similarly, from ruin, order is born; from order, virtue; and from virtue, glory and good fortune.

Past dynasties, civilizations, and progressive societies follow closely the historically recurrent pattern of ten-generation cycles.

No matter the advances in communications, technology, and weaponry, each takes the same course: Outburst to Conquest to Commerce to Affluence to Intellect to Decadence. Some disappear, as did Assyria and Etruria, while others, such as Egypt, Greece, Italy, Spain, and England, become backwater countries drawing tourists to view relics of their former glory.

The first accounting of ten-generation cycles appears in the Bible. Genesis 5:1 begins, "This is the book of the generations of Adam." The following thirty-one verses present the generational outline of Adam through Noah. This selective list of ten generations is recorded for the purpose of tracing the ancestry of Abraham. Thus, Genesis 11:10 begins, "These are the generations of Shem" and continues through Genesis 11:26 for another ten generations, ending with Abram (Abraham).

*   *   *   *

During America's Age of Decadence, I chronicled in *Mothers, Leadership, and Success, Book Two* an account of the United States from its humble beginning in 1763 to the year 1989. I will not tire you with statistics related to the nation's ascent and decline during those 226 years. The following tables, which summarize America's first ten-generation cycle, will acquaint you with the adherence of the Republic of the United States to this historical pattern. But first, a starting date is needed to analyze America's ten-generation cycle.

1776? That year of the signing of the Declaration of Independence represents the nation's political birth. The fight for independence, however, had begun at Lexington and Concord in 1775, and the First Continental Congress had already convened at Philadelphia in 1774. But early demonstrations against British control, including the Boston Massacre in 1770 and the Boston Tea Party in 1773, indicate that the social and cultural makeup of the United States was firmly established before any of these dates. So what is the earliest date for American society as it currently exists?

The year 1763 is a logical beginning date for the United States as a nation. Two events that year precipitated a change in perspective concerning the thirteen colonies by both the British crown and the colonists themselves.

In 1763 the Treaty of Paris ended the French and Indian War, an extension of the European Seven Years' War in which the colonists fought on behalf of Great Britain — the last stand taken by the colonists for the British. Also, the British Proclamation of 1763 drew an absolute, map-marked boundary beyond which any further westward movement by British subjects was prohibited. The colonies had been individually created and colonized through royal grants and each was subject to royal rule. In most cases, they had been treated as separate entities by British political and private agencies. By setting forth one boundary for all, the Proclamation of 1763 recognized and treated the thirteen colonies as a single unit.

Thus I consider 1763 to be the date of origin of the country as we know it today. Table 1 sets forth the Ages of the Republic of the United States.

Table 2 presents the birth generations for the United States since 1763. (A twenty-five-year span is used to denote a generation and to distinguish each birth generation of individuals growing up at the same time. Twenty-five years is the most accepted period to determine the length of a generation.)

With 1763 as the de facto beginning of the United States, 1998 became the tenth year of its tenth birth generation. Table 3 summarizes the seventh through the tenth birth generations and the ninth and tenth accomplishing generations, completing a ten-generation period (250 years) for the United States. Since the accomplishing age of individuals can also be termed a generation, an accomplishing generation is the twenty-five-year span during which the group members are ages thirty-six through sixty. This age group consistently makes the greatest contributions to a country's growth, improvement, well-being, and change. There are exceptions of course (certainly contributions are made by individuals under thirty-six and over sixty); nonetheless, the most changes, good or bad, in any given twenty-five-year period come from the thirty-six-through-sixty age group.

Table 4, which identifies U.S. presidents by accomplishing generations, indicates, often dramatically, differences in national priorities and the quality of presidential leadership from the first of one to the first of the next accomplishing generation, as found be-

[TABLE 1]
The Republic of the United States of America

Age of Outburst	1763–1890
Age of Conquest	1846–1933
Age of Commerce	1874–1971
Age of Affluence	1946–ca. 2000
Age of Intellect	1964–ca. 2006
Age of Decadence	1964–ca. 2012

[TABLE 2]
Birth Generations

Born	Generation
1738–1762	last British colonial
1763–1787	First
1788–1812	Second
1813–1837	Third
1838–1862	Fourth
1863–1887	Fifth
1888–1912	Sixth
1913–1937	Seventh
1938–1962	Eighth
1963–1987	Ninth
1988–2012	Tenth

[TABLE 3]
Birth and Accomplishing Generations

Birth Generation	Years of Birth
Tenth	1988–2012
Ninth	1963–1987
Eighth	1938–1962
Seventh	1913–1937

Accomplishing Generation	Years of Birth
Tenth (Generation X)	1952–1976
Ninth	1927–1951

[TABLE 4]
Presidents of the United States

Accomplishing Generation	Born	Presidents
First	1727–1751	George Washington, John Adams, Thomas Jefferson, James Madison
Second	1752–1776	James Monroe, John Quincy Adams, Andrew Jackson, Martin Van Buren (b. 1782), William Harrison
Third	1777–1801	John Tyler, James Polk, Zachary Taylor, Millard Fillmore, Franklin Pierce (b. 1804), James Buchanan
Fourth	1802–1826	Abraham Lincoln, Andrew Johnson, Ulysses Grant, Rutherford Hayes
Fifth	1827–1851	James Garfield, Chester Arthur, Grover Cleveland, Benjamin Harrison, Grover Cleveland (2nd term), William McKinley
Sixth	1852–1876	Theodore Roosevelt, William Taft, Woodrow Wilson, Warren Harding, Calvin Coolidge, Herbert Hoover
Seventh	1877–1901	Franklin Roosevelt, Harry Truman, Dwight Eisenhower
Eighth	1902–1926	John Kennedy, Lyndon Johnson, Richard Nixon, Gerald Ford, James Carter, Ronald Reagan, George Bush
Ninth	1927–1951	William Clinton
Tenth	1952–1976	

tween Abraham Lincoln and James Garfield. Significant differences also appear between the administrations that begin and end each presidential accomplishing generation, such as between John Tyler and James Buchanan, Theodore Roosevelt and Herbert Hoover, and John Kennedy and George Bush. Perhaps the differences result more from cyclical timing and changing public values than quality of leadership.

*   *   *   *

It is the tenth generation that merits your attention most. Before people understood the ten-generation cycles of civilizations, mystery shrouded the events of the twenty-five years of the tenth generation that ended each epoch. Famines, floods, hurricanes, blizzards, earthquakes, volcanic eruptions, outbreaks of disease, and other natural catastrophes seemed to bring about each era's end. Since decadence characterizes each tenth generation, many contemporaries believed that this or that god was using nature to punish the country for its evil ways. Even in my time, more than a few embrace this belief.

During the tenth generation of each advanced society, nature's assaults are little different than during each of the previous nine generations. When the society is young and vigorous, natural catastrophes are taken in stride; the people are resilient and able to overcome hardships. For instance, the 1900 hurricane that hit Galveston, Texas, took some six thousand lives and destroyed the city. With Red Cross assistance and private charity, the survivors endured. The found dead were buried and the city was rebuilt without federal funds. By contrast, since 1988, the first year of our nation's tenth generation, Americans have shown little self-reliance or ability to cope with natural disasters. On August 23, 1992, a 140-mile-per-hour-winds hurricane struck south Dade County, Florida, centering on Homestead. Inhabitants, paralyzed by inertia, waited for the federal government and the state of Florida to provide sustenance and shelter. Although unprecedented funds poured into rebuilding the devastated area, hurricane victims became angry and frustrated when the federal government took four days to respond.

President George Bush visited Homestead the following month and, a few days later, so did Vice President Dan Quayle. A year later, President William Clinton made the same journey to Homestead. Each promised more assistance and more money. Further, even though only nine lives were lost, the thousands of "survivors" were praised for their courage and their forbearance of the federal government's slowness in providing for their comfort — in

[TABLE 5]

The Great Civilizations' Tenth Generations

Civilization	Rise and Fall	Duration in Years	Tenth Generation
Assyria	859–612 B.C.	247	637–612 B.C.
Persia: Cyrus and his descendants	538–330 B.C.	208	355–330 B.C.
Greece: Alexander and his successors	331–100 B.C.	231	125–100 B.C.
Roman Republic	260–27 B.C.	233	52–27 B.C.
Roman Empire	27 B.C.–A.D. 180	207	A.D. 155–180
Arab Empire	634–880	246	855–880
Mameluke Empire	1250–1517	267	1492–1517
Ottoman Empire	1320–1570	250	1545–1570
Japan: Muromachi (or Ashikago) Shogunate	1333–1600	267	1575–1600
China: Ming Dynasty	1368–1644	276	1619–1644
Spain	1500–1750	250	1725–1750
Japan: Tokugawa Shogunate	1600–1867	267	1842–1867
China: Ch'ing (Manchu) Dynasty	1644–1911	267	1886–1911
Romanov Russia	1682–1916	234	1891–1916
British Empire	1700–1950	250	1925–1950
United States of America	1763–ca. 2012	ca. 250	1988–ca. 2012

providing for those who would not fend for themselves or move on to other areas for employment. A cynic could compare the 1900 Galveston and the 1992 Homestead hurricanes and conclude that more deaths mean fewer destitute survivors needing relief and help in rebuilding.

During the tenth generation, nothing high-minded remains of the civilization's vigorous and boundless beginning. Civilizations in decline are not unlike the elderly, ravaged by the same bacterial infections or viral invasions that their immune systems easily vanquished in their youth. Troubles, travails, tragedies mark the end of each great epoch. Corrupt and decadent leaders squabble over the remains of the rotting corpse of society. Good and honest men suffer intolerable experiences during the end of each era, their losses measured only in degree — livelihood or life.

This generation invariably spawns movements to make changes within the existing regime. Led by late-awakening people and a few politicians, these advocates advance reform, not revolution. The Ch'ing (Manchu) Dynasty, for example, ruled China for ten generations, from 1644 to 1911. On June 11, 1898, Emperor Kuang Hsu issued his first reform decree, which began the Hundred Days Reform. Over the next 102 days, the emperor issued some fifty reform edicts affecting government administration, military development, industry, education, and international relations. The Hundred Days Reform of 1898 failed; the dynasty collapsed thirteen years later. Similarly, for ten generations, from 1600 to 1867, the Tokugawa shogunate controlled Japan. Massive reforms were implemented by the chief senior councillor, Tadakuni, from 1841 to 1843. The cure failed, as did the Tokugawa shogunate a generation later.

And during the ten-generation reign of the Romanov tsars over Russia, from 1682 to 1916, liberal *zemstvos* attempted unsuccessfully to deliver relief from the laws of the tsar. But it was not until the tenth generation that reformers brought the then-split *zemstvo* factions into a coherent movement that in 1906 produced a duma. The legislative body, however, was ineffective. Although hated by the tsar, the reformers continued their efforts to effect change and retain the monarch. Romanov Russia failed eleven years later. The reform leaders, along with the tsar, left the land of the living when Lenin, Russia's "man on horseback," prevailed.

America's tenth-generation voters also clamored for major social changes in 1994. Copying Manchu emperor Kuang Hsu's Hundred Days Reform, cautious conservatives led the 1995 congressional reform movement under the banner of a "One Hundred Day Contract with America." The cry of Republican politicians for change inspired hope among domestic and foreign investors, which helped keep the cork in the financial bottle for several years. At the same time, political debate provoked a violent backlash from liberals who viewed the reforms as dangerous to their existence. The reforms, never delivered, followed history's well-worn path. They failed. Too little, too late.

Throughout history, without exception, tenth-generation reform fails. Reformers fail because all misdiagnose the illness. Each group sees a cancer that can be treated with reform, but none realizes that the cancer has metastasized.

Late-twentieth-century American reformers hoped to save the population of the United States as a whole, but the country was too disobedient, degenerate, and violent for salvation. And as all failed civilizations contained some good and honest people at the end, so too did the United States of America — its middle class being the last bastion of virtue, talent, learning, and religion. Only the middle class was respectable. But as the two extremes of American society — the corrupt and the violent — continue to expand, the middle class shrinks.

The righteous remnant of the middle class, the true America-within-America, realized, finally, that the nation as a whole could not be saved. This moral minority eventually became more concerned with building a new America than with the fate of the doomed majority. And it supported you to reverse the course of our stricken nation.

So as with all great nations, our country has repeated the historical, worldwide law of ten generations and thus made your emergence real. America's second ten-generation cycle, Empire, begins with your advent.

THE decline of the nation to the sad condition that you must now redress began in 1946 with the onset of the Age of Affluence. How did the United States stand as a nation in 1945? It stood alone at the top in wealth, power, and fame. The government owned 60 percent of the total gold held by world governments. The country had a military-industrial complex second to none and was the world's major oil exporter. It was the sole owner of the most powerful weapon in history, the atomic bomb. The work force had power; 36 percent of American workers belonged to unions. Business failures numbered only four per ten thousand firms, the lowest in American history. (The failure rate in 1932 was 154 per ten thousand companies; in 1985, 114 per ten thousand.)

In 1945, citizens, on the whole, were honest, moral, ethical, and law abiding. Good manners were expected; wholesale rudeness had not begun. Discipline and integrity were practiced and respected. A man's word was better than a contract. Borrowers and lenders expected loans to be repaid and almost all were. Buyers were treated as customers not as consumers. Personal savings were in; bankruptcy was a humiliation. Heroes were everywhere. Stealing or moral turpitude or plagiarism were called wrong, not a mistake. Criminals received little sympathy. "Malpractice" was a seldom-used word; "deferred adjudication" was a little-known phrase in criminal justice proceedings.

Perhaps 1945 was the true "high noon" of the United States. With the lifting of controls at the war's end, prices skyrocketed. People wanted to buy; they had money available from savings, but goods were scarce. The lean war years coming on the heels of the Great Depression and the money saved during the war welcomed in the Age of Affluence.

For the next seventeen years, 1946–1963, the descent from greatness was imperceptible. Indeed, the years from 1946 through 1963 were truly golden for the United States. But those seeds of affluence planted in 1946 sprouted in 1964.

One of the most visible ills of affluence was the kudzu-like spread of extreme obesity and anorexic thinness after 1964. While one group gorged, the other starved itself. Both were expressions of the same problem. Neither the grossly overweight nor the fleshless were concerned with real achievements in their lives. Affluence, low self-esteem, and an absence of physical labor in primarily nonachieving people brought about strange human configurations. In almost all earlier successful civilizations, overweight people were considered attractive. Plumpness indicated wealth, success, good temper, eminence for men, and sexuality and fertility for women. Even then, however, extreme obesity and abnormal thinness were considered freakish.

During my childhood in the 1930s, extreme obesity was rare. Good manners dictated that one not stare, as such a person was afflicted with a "glandular" problem. Carnivals provided a place to view those who were different. "Geeks," often alcoholics, were dressed in animal skins and gainfully employed to shriek, babble, and bite the heads off live chickens as a means of enticing the crowd to the ticket booth. For a small coin one could view the "fat lady" and the living "human skeleton" without being rude. "Anorexia" and "bulimia" were foreign terms in this era. By the 1990s, however, no one would pay to see a "fat lady" or a "human skeleton," as the grossly misproportioned were commonplace. Children no longer stared at the extremely obese; since, little different than their parents, they were accustomed to seeing such people.

Entrepreneurs capitalized on this American phenomenon. "All you can eat" restaurants became "troughs" of choice for the fast-growing corpulent consumers of calories. Virtually unbreakable chairs, designed to support a quarter of a ton, prevented many a lawsuit. With round, serious faces and plates towering with eatables, the gross worked hard to extend their skin. Already the body's largest organ, it was stretched further to cover bizarre positioning of globs of new fat. (In one establishment, I saw a man and woman each use two chairs to support their bulk, which would have dangerously overlapped a single chair.) The most unusual portion of this immense partaking of food was not in the thousands of calories consumed or the strange seating arrangement; it was that no one paid them a whit of attention, not even ill-mannered children seated nearby.

The United States government dictated that employers hire these food-driven people without discrimination. The excessively obese and painfully thin joined the indolent and mentally dull, fully protected from the needs of government and business to hire the most competent employees. Public school systems were ordered to hire these types. They became the examples for school-children to follow, and they did.

Lawmakers, quacks, and television programs transformed self-indulgent social behavior into diseases and genetic "predisposition to" disorders, thus removing personal responsibility. Individual accountability for gorging on high-fat foods was ignored and replaced by a *Tillandsia usneoides* (Spanish moss) mentality — that is, growing from airborne particles and water alone. It was decided that one's genes predisposed one to obesity, not the number of calories consumed. Similarly, anorexia and bulimia were viewed solely as eating disorders, divorced from personal accountability and an unwillingness to work. While many acutely obese humans lard themselves to the extent that their locomotive abilities are impaired, self-starved human beings do not have the energy to work.

But the meandering of these overfed and underfed people into America's mainstream is only coincidental to the most important social change that took place during the Age of Affluence — dominant, achieving women avoiding procreation and child rearing.

CHAPTER THREE

America's Accelerating Decline

Beginning in 1946, many dominant women with strong needs for achievement chose a life of accomplishment outside the home over motherhood. While the world's then-largest baby boom, 1946–1963, produced 76 million American children, there were actually fewer children destined for success. Child-rearing practices did not change in 1946; rather, high-achieving (dominant) mothers were having fewer or no children while low-achieving (nondominant) mothers were bearing and rearing our country's succeeding generations. Few Americans noted the missing (because unborn) achievement-oriented children until 1964, the year (when those born in 1946 turned eighteen) that ushered in the Age of Decadence.

America's general public was confounded by the events of 1964 and subsequent years. For instance, the sexual content of our culture changed more after 1964 than in the previous two centuries combined. Politicians knew better. They grasped the significance of Beatlemania, protests, riots, and 1000-fathom-curve cultural sea changes. Politicians competed among themselves to repudiate laws governing behavior. Immediate gratification, stealing, drug abuse, the breakup of the family, and acceptance of criminal looting in disregard of property rights were all embraced by knowledgeable politicians and many federal judges. Opinion-makers followed the lawmakers in rushing to ride the disobedient, lawbreaking wave of the future.

During this period, more dominant women embraced their new freedom to achieve success outside the home. These women, whose maternal ancestors nurtured the builders of a splendid America, reared still fewer children while competing with men in business, politics, law, and medicine. These outstanding women became examples for others to emulate. But where in an earlier America dominant sons of dominant mothers flowed into the leadership of mainstream America, by 1988 the flow had become barely a drip.

(Coincidental with the withholding of children by dominant women, more Americans would rather adopt a canine puppy than a human child.)

Every great civilization in recorded history, once it attained affluence, followed the same pattern of lower birth rates among dominant women. And, ironically, since the dominance trait is gender neutral, this trend of success outside the home by dominant women faded away for the same reason: successful women failed to issue and rear sufficient replacements.

Whether the general public realized this at the time is immaterial — it happened. What is germane, and to you especially, is that the majority of officeholders were conscious of the decreasing numbers of high achievers in our society. They capitalized on the ease of manipulating a larger percentage of low achievers in a decadent America than a like proportion of high achievers in an honest America. Lawmakers knew that the average person's ability to control the conditions of his life would decrease, but they were unconcerned. Instead they worked hard to find dupes. This is why politicians could never look at one another without laughing; each knew the other shared an equal interest in presenting a pompous public countenance to give importance to the deceits they perpetrated.

However, some Americans of my time saw officeholders as concerned only with immediate popularity and winning the next election. They believed that many politicians were neither intelligent nor farsighted enough to plan consciously for long-term manipulation of our culture.

In acts of propitiation, the sheep among the political schemers adopted the mannerisms, haircuts, attire, and demeanor of the counterculture of 1964. Concerned with winning the next election, they lacked the will to do otherwise. Whether done blindly to gain votes or knowingly to control the populace, politicians espoused the mores of decadence and dismantled the values of an earlier and more responsible America.

They enacted laws to strip away the tradition of family and parental accountability. American society accepted impregnation without accountability. A father could, because penalties were not enforced, dispute paternity, reject responsibility for his issue, or both. Maternity could not be denied, but child rearing could be ignored. Children "raised" themselves. Even though every mentally healthy child, regardless of ethnicity, has the capacity to be a genius, many of these disobedient, ignorant, and often violent products of procreation fulfilled the maxim that "The richest soil, if uncultivated, produces the rankest weeds."

Multiplying exponentially, these weed-children were foisted on the public school system. School boards armed with federal mandates pushed the near-impossible task of education onto unsuspecting school superintendents. Thus, child-rearing duties, started six years too late, were shifted adroitly from derelict families to foolish school superintendents. Public school administrators became political puppets for their school boards or naive proponents of the hopeless quest for a college education for all.

Dependent on enrollment for their existence, marginal colleges promoted the idea that public schools should be judged by the percentage of students graduated instead of by academic performance. At the insistence of politicians, public schools set goals to eliminate "dropouts," thereby increasing the flow to colleges. American officeholders knew that successful societies from the past also catered to the unlearned by creating undemanding universities for dunces who could not benefit from advanced education. Politicians, pretending that education and intelligence were synonymous, poured taxpayer money into a vast network of new colleges. Thus, affluence combined with lack of intelligence spawned the idea of advanced education for all. Mindless school curricula helped graduate illiterate primary and secondary students. In 1995, the College Board, administrator of the Scholastic Aptitude Test, joined the academic charade by devaluing its test questions. And to sustain enrollment, colleges offered remedial classes for those who could not read and write or add and subtract.

Reacting to debased education and the violence prevalent at public schools, a few families began educating their children at home. Home schooling did not involve sacrifice; these parents set a higher value on their children's futures than on a second income. Even though many home-schoolers, particularly mothers, were devout Christians and patriotic Americans, state governments, backed by public schoolteacher associations and working mothers, maneuvered to derail the home-schooling movement. Politicians knew that the successes of children taught at home by mothers without a college degree in education would expose to all the failure of tax-financed public schools. State legislators tried to destroy the home-schooling movement but failed. The numbers of home-schoolers increased as home schooling became the fastest-growing segment of American education.

Beginning in 1964, American English was attacked. First it was fractured, then butchered, and finally neutered. An archive of adverbs dominated television and radio. "Basically" prefaced sentences when the speaker was unsure of the truth. "Hopefully" became a euphemism for desperation. Weak, unsupported, and many times false statements were saturated with the word "fact" — "a matter of fact," "the fact is," "it is a fact," "in fact," "the fact of the matter," "a number of facts." The ignorant adopted "you know" and "like" as fillers to string words together, to fabricate meaningless sentences. And many ethnic leaders hailed street language and dialect as "heritage" and "culture," as acceptable as, or even preferable to, standard American English. It was easier to legitimize and then teach dialect than to change the child-rearing practices that perpetuated bad grammar and ignorance.

Television and film offered increasingly more portrayals of graphic violence, thus providing ideas for mayhem and murder, since many viewers lacked sufficient intelligence to separate illusion from reality.

The country's reverence of entertainers was characteristic of

America's exploding population of nondominant people. A talk-show host was the highest-paid amuser in 1994–1995, grossing for those two years 425,000 gold ounces. Although dominant, Oprah Winfrey was no more so than any president of the United States, yet she made more in those two years than did all forty-two American presidents combined in 206 years.

*   *   *   *

Converting the paper currency of my day to troy ounces of gold provides a more constant comparison of value over time. All governments throughout history debase their currency, whether metal or paper, to conceal a decline in affluence. Only their methods differ.

Ten generations before Christ, during the latter days of the Roman Republic, the silver content of the denarius was periodically reduced by adding alloy, and the aureus gold coin continued to shrink in size. In the latter days of the United States Republic, the government debased paper currency by exorbitant borrowing and deficit spending. The eroding value of the dollar makes earlier cost relationships based on the dollar without merit to my time and useless at your juncture.

Notwithstanding one to five year aberrations, both up and down, the value of gold inversely tracks, often precisely, the percentage of dollar debasement. Lawmakers were particularly devious in preventing the free exchange of dollars for gold and gold for dollars. Politicians knew full well that if dollars were freely convertible to gold, it would give their game away.

In my time, up to a 39-percent tax was assessed on each seemingly profitable gold transaction. No matter how high the value of gold rose in a year, only a portion of its inflated value was recoverable after taxation. This tax eliminated the dollar debasement safety of gold ownership. But only to a point. Once Americans realized that inflation neither would nor could be controlled, gold ownership and tax avoidance became prevalent. Fearing financial ruin, the prudent became dishonest.

Lawmakers lulled many Americans fearful of inflation with "inflation-proof bonds." Taxation on the inflation portion of these bonds negated protection against inflation. Further, the bonds were registered in the name of the purchaser, making tax collection easier.

Politicians were ready to defend the dollar — first, they would threaten to sell the nation's treasury of gold bullion. This would hold down the value of gold temporarily. When, finally, the sale of government-owned gold bullion began, foreigners would compete with Americans to buy the country's gold reserves, the last vestige of American stability. Even in my time, the national debt was beyond repayment and therefore ignored.

Lawmakers refused to give up; they continued their irresponsible ways. Following the lead of fiscally unsound countries in recent history, politicians had a remedy against the time when American citizens would become desperate for the financial safety of foreign currency. Laws controlling currency exchange and the amount of money that Americans could legally take out of the country were waiting to be implemented.

*   *   *   *

Throughout history public servants of failed civilizations distributed public largess during periods of affluence through welfare to the indolent and shiftless in order to buy their votes and attempt to purchase civil peace.

Lawmakers knew full well the consequences of "free" advanced education and government-funded "free" medical treatment for the poor. History abounds with examples. The first free public hospital was opened in Baghdad in the reign of Harun Al-Rashid, A.D. 786–809. During the reign of his son, Mamun, free public hospitals covered the Arab world from Spain to what is now Pakistan. The decadent and bankrupt Arab empire collapsed in A.D. 880, and its free public hospitals disappeared.

History reminded politicians that disposing of a country's wealth in this fashion did not originate in the United States. Not only were there historical precedents for their actions, they knew also from history that when previous civilizations followed this course, they failed, and such edifices crumbled. Lawmakers, while bestowing the earnings of the hardworking on the undeserving, knew that it was only a matter of time before the economy of the United States could no longer sustain such benevolence. They knew that most American colleges would close and hospitals would follow to ruin. Still, without compunction they deceived hardworking Americans and bankrupted the country.

AFTER 1964, politicians encouraged the formation of activist organizations with agendas that would not threaten their political well-being. The soft-hearted view all evils as equally noxious; they rail against secondhand smoke with the same fervor as against murder. Animal rights groups protected the rights of animals so as to prevent human exploitation and physical abuse. At the same time, other activists agitated for the rights of the worst human "animals," abusers and murderers of other human beings, by slowing, then halting, imprisonment and execution.

In turn, politicians felt threatened when groups of citizens opposed to decadence and vacuous government emerged. Among these were devoutly religious families that banded together in rural areas in an attempt to regain control of their day-to-day living. These groups, labeled "militia" and "survivalists," were made uneasy by the decadence surrounding them and were confounded by laws that left criminals unpunished and special minorities rewarded unduly. They shared two beliefs: the most fundamental was a distrust of the federal government; the other, a fear of personal injustice at the hands of government. Alarmed by increasing national lawlessness, these groups considered themselves bastions of a long ago, self-sufficient America.

Following the lead of political and media propaganda, however, the general public lumped these clusters of militia and survivalists in the same evil bracket as groups of hatemongers and loners who committed terrorist acts. While a handful of militia and survivalist members did commit despicable acts, and more than a few were dishonest, the majority were politically unambitious, hardworking, decent Americans seeking only to be left alone and not oppressed.

Fueled by a fear of rebellion or uprising, the wrath of the failing federal government sometimes delivered unjust acts upon militia and survivalist adherents — the very people most fearful of injustice — thus making the circle complete. Still, their numbers grew.

O F course some politicians worked diligently to prevent laws designed to break America. These lawmakers were few, and, alas, their names are commingled and lost along with those of their deceitful and more prosperous colleagues. Mixed among the few builders and the many destroyers were would-be statesmen, clever but not bright. As H. G. Wells wrote, "The last thing they wanted to do was to penetrate below the surface of things on which they lived so agreeably."

Politicians did not unwittingly make stupid mistakes. On the contrary, these were calculated decisions made by bright people with other agendas. Many politicians will do anything to satisfy their needs to be loved, to be idolized, to be godlike, including pandering to voters for election and reelection. More than a few Americans believed that most incumbent lawmakers and their appointed federal judges knew — even though they pretended not to — at the time of their actions just how their decisions would humble the United States.

It could be, of course, that the actions of the agents of decline were historically inevitable. Whether the destruction was witting or unintentional matters little. Congressional officeholders were worse than the slimy incubi of earlier times. At the same time, they exploited and gulled honest, though gullible, Americans. Politicians had become pimps for a decadent America.

CHAPTER FOUR

Flatulence and Mendacity

O ne of civilization's strange quirks is the embarrassment associated with the expulsion of bodily gases, particularly in the
presence of members of the opposite sex. Some feel shame for ex-
pelling lower intestinal gas in mixed company. Some see dishonor
in telling lies. And then there are politicians. . . . They fear ex-
pelling body gases in public yet relish telling lies. This is strange indeed: the concentration needed to constrict one's sphincter muscle
is far greater than that required to keep one's mouth closed. But
while flatus is a natural bodily function, mendacity is an acquired
habit.

When making determinations, it is usually best to think in degrees rather than absolutes; when dealing with flatulence and
mendacity, however, degrees are unnecessary. Either a person did
or did not publicly expel body gases; either a person did or did not
tell a lie.

As with any form of self-consciousness, memories endure and
stories hold sway for decades, even centuries. Three stories illustrate concern over flatulence transformed into jest: first, an Arab
tale from *Mr. "J"*; second, William Safire's version of a story that
President Abraham Lincoln enjoyed telling; and third, an Eliza-
bethan anecdote retold by Will Durant.

Muza Dai Boo, an Arab merchant, was in the marketplace one day when he felt terrible cramps. He just couldn't control himself, and let out a long, loud fart.

People stared at him from all sides. Mortally embarrassed, he ran back to his home, packed his few belongings and journeyed far away. For years he traveled from town to town, but always avoided his home town.

At last, an old and weary man, he decided to return. He had grown a long beard and his face had aged enough so that he was sure he would not be recognized. His heart longed for the old familiar streets.

Once in town, he went directly to the marketplace. There, to his surprise, he saw that the street had been paved. He turned to the man nearest him and said, "My friend, how smooth this street is. When, by the grave of Allah, was it so neatly paved?"

"Oh, that," said the man. "That was done three years, four months and two days after Muza Dai Boo farted in the marketplace."

*

There was a party once, not far from Springfield, and among the crowd was one of those men who had audacity. Cheeky, quick-witted, never off guard on any occasion. The audacious man, chosen to be the carver of the turkey at the dinner table, whetted his great carving knife and got down to business carving the bird.

The man of audacity expended too much force and let a fart, a loud fart, so that all the people heard it distinctly. It shocked all. A deep silence reigned.

However, the audacious man was entirely self-possessed. He pulled off his coat, rolled up his sleeves, spat on his hands, whetted the carving knife again, never cracking a smile or moving a muscle on his face. It became a wonder in the minds of all the men and women how the fellow was to get out of his dilemma.

He squared himself and said loudly and distinctly, "Now, by God, I'll see if I can't cut up this turkey without farting!"

*

Edward de Vere, Earle of Oxford, making his low obeisance to Queen Elizabeth, happened to let a Fart, at which he was so abashed and ashamed that he went to Travell, 7 yeares. On his returne the Queen welcomed him home, and sayd, My Lord, I had forgott the Fart.

While disliking to expel bodily gases in public, honest people will always choose to let a fart rather than tell a lie. Politicians, devoid of the truth, have a horror of letting a public fart, but they crave audiences to which they can tell lies. It is just as rare to get a whiff of a truth from the lips of politicians as it is to hear them fart. Should you find some means of establishing public flatulence as acceptable without social penalty, and lies by politicians as unacceptable and punishable, the lawmakers of your time may exercise better control over the opening and closing of the larger orifice.

While no civilization is ever free from dishonest and corrupt politicians, the percentages of deceitful and mendacious politicians rise dramatically in the ninth and tenth generations of an epoch. After 1964, no American president dared tell Americans the truth about the state of the union, believing that the public lacked the courage to deal with bad news, or fearing that they would not be reelected unless they deemed the country to be doing well under their leadership. In their need to be revered and godlike, our politicians chose to emulate a loving, bestowing, and deceitful pagan god rather than modeling themselves after an honest, righteous, and sometimes wrathful God.

In this Age of Decadence, political and social sophists reign supreme. Rather than bother you with statistics, I merely list some examples of their chicanery. These items have no immediate use, but you may profit by taking an opposite course as similar situations arise.

Since 1964, as each respective bill passed into law, enough American lawmakers to constitute a majority knew when they voted how the cumulative effect would bring harm to the United States. While practicing their dangerous dodges and deceits, politicians knew the following while pretending they did not:

- Dozens of laws took what were once moral problems and redefined them as either diseases or genetically uncontrollable behaviors.

- Overt homosexuality is rampant near the end of all ten-generation cycles.
- During the five to six generations it takes for a lethal infection to adapt a sustained tolerance to a new virus, thousands of innocent Americans would die from Acquired Immune Deficiency Syndrome, *Slim* (Uganda, considered by many to be the cradle of AIDS, developed several descriptive terms for the disease: *Gongo, Lumalabantu, Mukenenya, Slimu,* and *Slim*).
- Periodic nationwide blood testing and quarantine of Human Immunodeficiency Virus carriers could prevent more than 90 percent of new *Slim* occurrences.
- Any difference in lower intelligence of Negroes versus Caucasians was attributable directly to child-rearing practices and not to genetics, past slavery, or discrimination.
- Slavery, having existed as long as recorded history, could well have been a reality for over a million years; thus, every person living today, regardless of race and ethnicity, has slave ancestors.
- Race riots and civil unrest would occur simultaneously nationwide.
- Hiring less-qualified postal employees through "race norming" would ruin the United States Postal Service.
- Providing welfare, without work, to able-bodied citizens would weaken the ability of the recipients to provide for themselves and would create fierce infighting among themselves, little different from the continuous feeding of animals in the wild.
- Monthly cash payments for children without fathers would create a strong reason for indolent women and young girls to labor issuing children for pay rather than working in industry for money.

Lawmakers were mindful that

- Granting amnesty to millions of Hispanic aliens living illegally in the United States would not stem the tide of new illegal immigrants; instead, it would tax municipal services and the welfare system.

- Thousands of American citizens would be burglarized, robbed, raped, and murdered by Mexican nationals who flee to Mexico for safety without concern of extradition.
- History records no successes in appeasement.
- Laws to prevent discrimination against broad categories of the handicapped — including the indolent, the extremely obese, and the mentally dull — would lead to the manufacturing of inferior goods or higher priced goods and the displacement of American jobs to countries that did discriminate.
- Any attempt to assist failing manufacturers by imposing import quotas on better-made or less-expensive foreign goods would fail due to discriminating demand for these goods by American consumers.
- Repeatedly shifting the base year to determine inflation and continually changing the inflation formulas would trick the public.
- Inflation would not be contained and hyperinflation would result.
- The major portion of annuities and pension funds invested with insurance firms would not be paid.
- Government-guaranteed loans, equal to the national deficit figure but not mentioned as a financial liability, would contribute to economic disaster.

Politicians knew that the time would come when:

- A value-added tax would be assessed and add to Americans' tax burden.
- State governments and municipalities would demand payment of property taxes a year in advance.
- Foreign investors would shun dollar-denominated debt except as rank speculation.
- The leaders of Arab oil-producing countries would not remain ignorant and eventually would base oil prices on another denominator instead of the dollar.
- Over half of the 3,280 colleges open in 1982, and a like percentage of hospitals, would fail and close their doors.

- The drastic percentage movement of funds from public elementary and secondary education to community colleges and universities would tear down America's educational system.
- General Motors Corporation would file for bankruptcy.
- The Tennessee Valley Authority's bonds scheduled to mature in 2042 would be worthless well in advance of their maturity.

Additionally, they were cognizant that

- Litigious attorneys were unjustly enriching themselves through the largest transfer of wealth in American history to my time.
- America's sports fanatics would maim and kill partisans of rival teams.
- Democracy in Russia would not prevail, and a dictator would reclaim most, if not all, lost territories.
- Democracy in South Africa would fail, and the Negro majority would first financially destroy the assets of the country and then physically harm the Caucasian population.

ON occasion political pretense failed. The hypocrisy of a gun-control agenda was seen through by too many to slip entirely into law. The ludicrousness of implementing such laws was evident in the nonenforcement of existing laws. (Gun-control laws in countries such as Sweden are superfluous, since all laws are enforced.)

Government gun control was a rotten political red herring, and most Americans could not ignore the smell. In 1994, by contrast, 6.2 million Americans used cocaine either once a week to every two weeks or so, more than 70 million citizens had smoked marijuana, and about 10 million continued to do so. Yet during 1994 only one criminal was jailed for every hundred violent crimes committed. Few American laws were enforced. And when a country cannot prosecute all enactments equally, implementing measures such as gun control simply serves notice that a nation is either fearful of its citizens or unable to enforce existing laws.

Still, for the most part, politicians rose to meet the challenge. Rather than stop crime, politicians recategorized crimes. In addition, comparisons to bygone days were eliminated by using new annual crime statistics. Each year politicians either congratulated themselves when crime decreased or excused an increase with reasons defying logic. Neither politicians nor law enforcement agencies dared use 1963, the year before America's Age of Decadence began, as the base year for determining the rate of growth in crime. They knew that single-year downturns in criminal activities would then reflect a minuscule blip in the ever-increasing crime rate. Victims and knowledgeable citizens knew the truth but were powerless to act.

UNCHALLENGED mendacity led to unbounded arrogance. The most powerful politicians could not get enough power, fame, or money, particularly money. Unfairly and unjustly, though legally, male members of Congress placed their wives in government positions of honor and high pay. Equally legal, though no less wrong, were the actions of other representatives and senators who secured employment and grand remunerations for their spouses at large corporations. Moreover, influential officeholders, upon leaving public office, indulged themselves with lucrative lobbying arrangements and pricey lecture tours. Greedy lawmakers left nothing on the table.

Politicians worshiped themselves first, last, and most of all. A popular catchphrase among them, "Not on my watch," expressed their contempt for the concerns of the nation, thinking it a clever joke to say that they did not care whether the ship sank, only that it sink while someone else was officially responsible. Among these facile lawmakers, fewer than a handful ever captained a ship.

After 1988, American leaders gorged as never before on the spoils available for the clever among the crooked, for the dishonest among the decadent. It mattered not to politicians that a thousand honest citizens suffered so that one dishonest politician might prosper. (No hardworking, honest citizen would entrust his personal assets or private business to the management of a politician, for he would be considered a fool by his fellow Americans.) When you are urged to temporize, think of the honest citizens violated throughout history during the tenth generation of their civilization, and then act accordingly.

Worst of all were the lawyer-congressmen who confused argument with bravery. In 1993, lawyers in the 103rd Congress numbered 239, almost one in two; only ten members of the House, and none in the Senate, had a law enforcement background; and only one senator, and no member of the House, was a military professional before election to Congress.

Just prior to your presidency, many believed that little in the nation would improve and much would worsen. Angry, dispirited people cry out for two things: a strong leader to follow and a scapegoat to blame. You are their strong leader; at the same time, only you can provide the needed scapegoat for them. You must choose the scapegoat; otherwise the people will fill the vacuum by selecting from an array of age-old scapegoats. Other authoritarian rulers pointed the finger of blame and hate at Jews, Catholics, Protestants, Muslims, Hindus, nonbelievers, Negroes, Caucasians, the elderly, the upper classes, and the lower classes. Resist personal preferences and the advice of others to designate any age, class, religion, or ethnicity as the scapegoat. You must harness the productive energies of the few remaining honest Americans with talent. You need them all. Perhaps the most deserving group to offer as a scapegoat is the politicians of your time. This choice frees you of ethnic, religious, class, and age discrimination.

In their blessed state, politicians, even more than low-class criminals, believe that "It won't happen to me." Further, when catastrophe strikes America because of their doing, they believe they can resign with honor should they be left holding the bag.

For example, each and every lawmaker spoke against "deficit spending" and for "balancing the budget." Still, they spent and spent. By focusing on annual deficits and not on government debt, shrewd politicians confused and lulled voters into believing that dire consequences would befall their children and grandchildren, though voters themselves would remain unharmed. Since few voters are farsighted enough to concern themselves with problems that might arise after their deaths, lawmakers held the potential outcry to a murmur. Politicians postponed the day of reckoning until the United States owed roughly as much as all the other countries of the world combined.

Americans were to be shocked, then enraged, when payment came due in their lifetimes. While the downtrodden rarely rise up in anger, it is different with people whose aroused expectations are extinguished; their fury cannot be placated. But passions and reactions differ. The most bitter are those who saved and hold near-worthless currency. The angriest are those among the unemployed who worked hard and practiced the work ethic since childhood. The indifferent are politicians and bureaucrats, since they have inflation-proof retirement benefits. The most harmed are the elderly on fixed incomes. The most violent are those on the dole whose welfare payments no longer sustain them without working. The most fearful are the wealthy; though financially safe, they fear for their lives.

As conflicting passions converge, doomed expectations move the wrathful from civil unrest, to turbulence, to violence, to anarchy, to America's Man on Horseback.

CHAPTER FIVE

Securing and Expanding Power

I can only imagine what a sorry lot of miscalculating rascals occupy the once-hallowed halls of Congress at your ascendancy. Fear not these knaves. Most will deliver masterful oratory while turning their coats to you. It is you, not they, who concern me.

Time is your enemy; it cannot be repossessed. Time spent consolidating power is the act of an unsure, timorous leader. Time spent placating the opposition or rewarding unqualified key supporters with political positions is opportunity wasted for an invincible leader. In my time, a hundred-day grace period was traditional; judgment was withheld somewhat for the first hundred days of a new presidency. Move quickly during this customary calm period.

In advising you and executing your orders, your cabinet will help you revitalize America and make whole again this great nation. Their titles matter little, whether seemingly broad or narrow in scope; ensure only that the titles give the appearance of tradition. In my time, cabinet heads numbered a cumbersome thirteen, plum political appointments all. Reduce their number to seven, and choose the members carefully. Disregard individual quirks of human nature. What matters are the ethics, intellect, and wisdom of those who counsel you and that they are tough-minded and courageous. Equally important is their desire to carry out your every decision without reluctance.

In times past, for the good of the country, it was better by far to choose unchaste but wise advisers, such as Benjamin Franklin, Alexander Hamilton, and Daniel Webster. In more recent times, neither those cast in the mold of the seemingly self-restrained Richard Nixon, who smiled little and whose word was of no account, nor the promiscuous William Clinton, who was a war avoider with the remarkable ability to smile even as he mourned, should be considered as possible advisers. Seek only those whose advice and actions will benefit the nation and you.

Ignore past friends for cabinet positions. Many times friendship is viewed as license to chastise. Moreover, the prerequisite for friendship is a mutual feeling of equality. You have no equals. Your friendships are those of utility; when the utility ceases, so does the friendship.

While six of your seven cabinet members must be people of inner strength, strong will, and honest counsel, the seventh should be a shallow flatterer of wit and guile. A flatterer is a secret enemy who will act as your lightning rod, drawing others of his ilk. He will become the ingratiating spokesman for your enemies. That he suggests false paths to you is irrelevant; before he can imitate Judas Iscariot, you will know your highest-placed adversaries. You need no advice from me to deal with this situation as it unwinds.

Accomplishment-oriented government, like progressive enterprises everywhere, dictates a small number of subordinates. Thus, I recommend that the seven key people reporting to you have a like number reporting to each of them, with the same traits as your best six.

Remember, any time spent grooming a successor is futile. At best, your heir apparent will be a yes-man; at worst, he will be drawn to your flatterer. Additionally, you will squander time defending his actions.

Defend no one. Each person must rise or fall based on performance alone. Your successor rises only when you fall. Should you fail, politicians will select a weak figurehead to replace you, a move that buys time for political compromise, power consolidation, and intrigue. Then, the rat with the longest tail will get the most syrup.

Each day expand your power; you have no time to waste consolidating power. We both know that you will suspend the U.S. Constitution and writ of habeas corpus, no matter my thoughts. I do not approve of sedition, but I believe that you are, as Michael J. Sandel wrote of "the man on horseback," "an authoritarian figure who offers a way beyond impasse, above politics, and beyond the messy, often frustrating restraints of constitutional government." And I recognize the perilous times our once-great nation faces. I suspect that you will use, as partial precedent, the actions of an earlier commander in chief, Abraham Lincoln. In dealing with persons suspected of treasonable intent, Lincoln at times authorized his generals to make arbitrary arrests. He justified this action on the ground that he had to allow some temporary sacrifice of parts of the Constitution in order to maintain the Union and thus preserve the Constitution as a whole.

The country during the American Civil War was divided between good men at cross-purposes. You, too, have war. At your presidency, you will find the country split between honest and dishonest men, between an embattled, despairing middle class and chaos. Given time, such chaotic conditions will focus America's hatred onto politicians. Reviled and spit on by constituents, few United States representatives or senators will dare visit their home districts.

But whether they love or hate you, congressional members and voters alike know that their alternative to you is a military triumvirate. Fearing military rule and drumhead justice on one side and wrathful citizens on the other, Congress awaits your summons and initiatives.

You promised America a real war against criminals. If you choose to ask for a declaration of war against crime, Congress will deliver. The declaration should remain in effect until you no longer need it; for, beneath its shelter of legality, you can expand its jurisdiction. Congressional usefulness ceases after producing the war declaration. (As history informs us, treason is never successful; for when treason triumphs, none dare call it treason.) But be prepared that, in the interest of national security, Congress and the Constitution may stand in the way of your goals.

Furthermore, as you know, for you to succeed, you must have more than just tacit support from all military leaders of consequence. Without fail, great leaders minister to the needs of the military, those serving and the veterans. Carry your esteem for America's armed forces further. Adopt as your personal cause the care of disabled veterans. This alone ensures large contributions from citizens who want your friendship. Do more. Give your worldly goods along with almost all your presidential pay to this foundation for disabled veterans. Keep for yourself only a sum equal to that of the nation's lowest-paid soldier. While appearing altruistic, this buys you an insurance policy with the armed forces at a small cost relative to its future benefits. While small-minded authoritarian leaders prepare for flight by amassing and secreting away (outside their nation) immense sums of gold to ease their transition from great power to comfortable exile, your act of giving serves notice that you are honest, love your veterans, have burned your personal boat, and are here to stay.

These actions, though commendable, will do nothing to silence your adversaries. When you suspend the Constitution and the writ of habeas corpus, enemies and their public statements of indignation will surface. Your supporters will record the names of those individuals, tape their television quotes, and fill electronic file cabinets with their newspaper articles — all of which can be of immense value to you in times ahead, as the names of your impulsive adversaries will be documented for future recall and consideration. Similarly, the carping of foreign heads of state, however strident, is not worth heeding, since you hold the trigger to America's weaponry. Though your military is a shadow of its former strength, its might remains the most formidable in the world. Foreign leaders, judging you solely by your predecessors, can be excused their initial stupidity. They will soon understand who you are.

The next step in your plan will be to exert control and decrease legislative power by increasing the number of traditional congressional positions, thereby reducing the power of each member more than just proportionately. In any endeavor, an extensive body is controlled more easily than an abbreviated one. Dilute your opposition but, for the sake of appearances, keep the framework of the Republic intact. Double the membership in the House of Representatives and the Senate. Maintain the same voting districts to preserve convention: have each district elect two representatives and each state four senators. Eliminate staggered terms for senate seats, thus ensuring complete congressional turnover every six years. At some time during your first hundred days in office, call for elections and require all seated members to stand for re-election.

Although decreasing individual power, adding positions will allow forthright Americans who believe that they can make a difference to involve themselves with changing government operations. Excited and inspired by your sweeping changes, honest Americans will compete with those incumbents motivated by unrequited needs to be godlike. More importantly, each congressional member will be forced either to resign or to struggle to keep his job and safeguard his perquisites. Should an adversary resign, his power goes also; if he stands for reelection, he shall be busy in his district and have little time to plot against you. Give them reasons to decline running for reelection. For example, before the elections, reduce total congressional funding by half (which will be halved again when twice as many congressional members occupy the same offices). Money will mean little to those who want desperately to join you and your fight for America's revival. Also, keep them busy. Charge the new Congress to concentrate on understanding and embodying the will of the people. Regardless of the election outcome, the sheer numbers of lawmakers prevent the cohesion necessary to rise against you.

With that in mind, should the United States Supreme Court seat nine members at your time, increase that number to fifteen. If the number is eleven, then increase it to nineteen. Numerous candidates who share your beliefs for restoring American justice will step forward.

Fortune smiles on the bold during crises. Repeal every federal, state, and local bill and statute that became law from 1964 on, along with all the ensuing regulations spawned from that period.

Americans of my time were burdened with 150,000 new laws and two million new regulations each and every year. Of course, among these thousands of bills, most of which helped devastate America while bringing pleasure and reelection to lawmakers, are a handful of beneficial statutes that you may wish to reinstate later. It is far easier to repeal all than debate a few. You have no time for debate.

Repealing these laws serves you mightily. Over five million bureaucrats and government consultants will be out of jobs, and many millions of welfare recipients will be off the dole, and all, as a consequence, will be running around willy-nilly seeking gainful employment. The equivalent of a half-billion ounces of gold stops its flow from the nation's treasury the first year. And with this drastic downsizing expect inflation to drop dramatically. You will be recognized as a resolute leader with a momentous purpose.

Y o u have accomplished much in a short time. Your position is strong, despite the many protests against your actions. The armed forces of the United States are on your side, and Congress is powerless without the Constitution.

Your possible peril lies in how well you chose your six cabinet members — do they have the wisdom and the will to execute your agenda to restore the United States to greatness? — and in how quickly you begin addressing the nation's problems: crime, financial chaos, ongoing riots, terrorism, and anarchy. Now is the time to unsheathe your plan for America's restoration. Communicate with candor, Mr. President. Resolve quickly your most distasteful agenda items. At the same time, assure Americans that you will give scrupulous attention to business, the economy, and charity and promise future full employment. Pledge to act with honesty and to reestablish democracy.

Today your enemies are the most numerous and vociferous. Ask God, in His providence, to sustain you and support you in your resolve. Your magnificent successes will carry you to great heights. But since triumphs cannot continue forever, be mindful that setbacks will occur and that there will be conspiracies against you. Take comfort in the words of Machiavelli: "as it often happens in conspiracies that few are not enough and many expose them."

And you have your flatterer in place. Now you are ready to fight crime.

But while you came to power because of crime and corruption, your true importance lies in introducing far-reaching changes that will move the United States to a glorious new ten-generation cycle. Empire!

[CHAPTER SIX]

A New Justice System

❧

Crime and punishment are sworn enemies. When one tri-umphs, the other loses; fairness rarely prevails. Perhaps Machiavelli would agree that criminals "want our persons and our substance so as to be able to satiate their cruelty with our blood and their avarice with our property." So a declaration of war on criminals will be your first test of presidential will. The country is anxious to learn of your methods and the depth of your resolve. Act now.

I have no doubt that you will win your first conflict in the war against crime, succeeding to the degree that you are inclined. Be-lieving that all criminal activities will increase tenfold from my time to yours, I anticipate what you face and surmise how many criminals will cease to exist during your first assault. Use haste, but you need not follow in the footsteps of Genghis Khan, who wanted slavery, not the goodwill of men. Nor should you imitate Mao Tse-tung, who while more subtle, fell many more than did the mighty Khan.

Mao Tse-tung, after overthrowing the drug-dealing Chiang Kai-shek in 1949, promulgated a nationwide edict: all users of illegal drugs must register for treatment within ninety days. After this grace period, any of the country's 538 million found with unlawful drugs in their possession were summarily executed. Mao's minions compiled lists of the names of unregistered illicit drug users. Wronged citizens gleefully passed along the names of attorneys, landlords, and the wealthy. Even descendants of generations-ago wrongdoers were named. Pent-up fury in China's masses capitalized on this opportunity to even new and old scores. Guilty or not, for right or wrong, many besides drug users became victims of this hysteria. It is estimated that more than seven million citizens were extinguished in this fashion, an unrecorded percentage of which were not actually users of prohibited drugs. (This represented only a small portion of Mao Tse-tung's thirty years of purges.) By the end of 1950, and during the following three decades of Mao's rule, had an unguarded mountain of heroin been placed in the center of Shanghai, it would have remained untouched by China's millions. So ended two hundred years of opium and heroin subjection for China's people.

In some Moslem cultures of my time — where the right hand is used for eating, many times from a communal pot, and the left hand is used for wiping after defecating — the initial penalty for selling forbidden drugs is removal of the right hand. No illegal drug problems exist in those realms. America has no kindred taboo of left hand use, however, and contains too large a population to enforce comparable rules.

But there are better ways to lay siege against the demand for illegal drugs in the United States. Eradicate drug abuse in a manner that will fit your bent toward benevolence and the rebuilding of America rather than reduce you to the role of a destructive despot.

I advocate that you promulgate new laws for crime and punishment to be in force well in advance of military deployment. First, eliminate the death penalty for capital murder. Second, incarcerate in doubling increments of two, four, eight, sixteen, and thirty-two years and eliminate parole, as such short sentences negate the need for it. Third, have set punishments for set crimes. And finally, change the age of adult accountability to thirteen.

Use America's communication systems to propagandize your new crime code. Appeal to the many who feel rather than the few who think, as most see reality with their feelings, not with logic.

Establish your humanitarianism by eliminating the death penalty and limiting prison terms, thus balancing your forthcoming ruthless war on terrorists, rioters, criminal gangs, and ochlocracy. Compassion dictates that you impose sentences no longer than thirty-two years. In addition, eliminating the death penalty will save a staggering sum of money; in 1994, the cost per execution was 6,000 gold ounces, much of which was pocketed by court-appointed lawyers.

Further, pierce the corporate veil and hold chief executive officers and board members personally liable for corporate criminal actions. As they are quick learners, illegal dumping of toxic wastes, theft of annuity funds, product price fixing, and corporate malfeasance will grind to a halt. Resentment from members of the establishment will smolder, but address that later.

But beware. Complicated, obtuse laws encourage criminal enterprises. Strangely enough, overly harsh laws have the same results. In 1689 England, crimes for which the statutory penalty was death numbered fifty. When criminals were drawn and quartered, great crowds of merrymakers attended the festivities. Cutpurses and thieves worked the crowds of gawking spectators, often committing transgressions greater than those perpetrated by the object of the throng's glee. In 1820, to better protect property rights, English courts increased the number of crimes calling for the death penalty to 160. Crime increased nevertheless.

Following England's example, in 1994 Congress passed, and President William Clinton signed into law, a crime bill that permitted the death penalty for sixty additional federal crimes. As with England in 1820, nothing changed.

As commander in chief, and with your declaration of war, nothing interferes with your actions against crime. Create a new system of trial, punishment, and imprisonment. It is far too late for reform or restructuring. The simplicity of the new system — set punishments for set crimes — eliminates the need for jury trials. Three-judge panels are ample. Your cabinet members' subordinates can select the necessary number of like-minded judges to initiate America's new criminal justice program. Should some prove ineffective, replace them. With preset sentences, judges need only determine guilt. (Paint stars from the United States flag on the ceilings of the judges' chambers to symbolize the righteousness of America's new judicial system.) Meaningful justice entails swift and sure judgment. Appeals are unnecessary with well-grounded adjudication.

In my time, capricious and arbitrary decisions were prohibited, while cruel and unusual punishment was debated without end. Sentencing became illogical. For example, rapists of my era received sentences of ninety-nine years. Some second- and third-offense rapist-murderers received prison time of greater lengths, such as three life sentences plus fifty years. Sentences exceeding three hundred years were not uncommon. One prison term of three thousand years infuriated the softhearted. In truth, incarceration for three thousand years would be harsh even in the time of Methuselah. Such lengthy, inhumane prison sentences led kindhearted politicians and parole boards to offer parole after a piddling number of years, sometimes months. When the parolee committed another heinous crime, a few jury sentences became merciless and longer, while actual time served became more merciful and shorter.

Mr. President, consider the following eight crime categories and corresponding punishments. Eight is sufficient. State crimes not listed will fit easily in one of these classifications. Punishment for federal crimes can be assessed conveniently within the five felony categories.

MISDEMEANOR

Class III:	Speeding and other minor traffic violations; burglary, theft, or criminal mischief where the amount of pecuniary loss is less than one-twentieth of an ounce of gold. **A fine of one ounce of gold.**
Class II:	Major traffic violations; burglary, theft, or criminal mischief where pecuniary loss is one-twentieth or more of an ounce of gold but less than one and one-quarter gold ounces. **One hundred eighty days confinement in the county jail and a fine of two ounces of gold.**
Class I:	Burglary, theft, or criminal mischief where the pecuniary loss is one and one-quarter or more gold ounces but less than four ounces of gold; simple assault when no serious

injury occurs; fleeing on foot from a peace officer; abuse and injury to livestock; driving while intoxicated.

One year confinement in the county jail and a fine of four ounces of gold.

FELONY

Fourth Degree: Burglary, theft, or criminal mischief where the amount of pecuniary loss is four or more ounces of gold but less than fifty gold ounces; criminal trespass; fleeing from a peace officer while driving a motor vehicle; possession of a controlled substance.
Two years prison confinement and a fine of eight ounces of gold.

Third Degree: Burglary, theft, or criminal mischief where the amount of pecuniary loss is fifty or more ounces of gold but less than 250 gold ounces; simple sexual assault; assault of a man upon a woman; disruption of government, school, or church meetings; causing injury of a person when fleeing from a peace officer while driving a motor vehicle; causing injury of a person when driving a motor vehicle while intoxicated; delivery of a controlled substance.
Four years confinement and a fine of sixteen ounces of gold.

Second Degree: Burglary, theft, or criminal mischief where the amount of pecuniary loss is 250 or more ounces of gold but less than 500 gold ounces; burglary of a building; assault where serious bodily injury occurs; assault on a police officer or fireman; assault in the course of escape or attempted escape from a United States penal institution; causing the death of a person when fleeing from a peace officer while driving a motor vehicle; causing the death of a person when driving a motor vehicle while intoxicated; delivery of a controlled substance to minors; sexual assault by someone thirteen or older on a person twelve years of age or younger.
Eight years confinement and a fine of sixteen ounces of gold.

First Degree: Murder; causing the death of a peace officer when fleeing from a peace officer while driving a motor vehicle;
robbery by use of a deadly weapon; aggravated sexual assault; aggravated kidnapping; arson; burglary, theft, or
criminal mischief where the amount of pecuniary loss is
500 or more ounces of gold.
**Sixteen years confinement and a fine of thirty-two
ounces of gold.**

Capital: Murder in the course of committing rape, robbery, kidnapping, or theft; murder of a peace officer; murder of a
fireman; murder of a public servant; murder of more
than one person in the same criminal episode; murder of
a person twelve years of age or younger by someone
thirteen or older; murder while in the course of escape or
attempted escape from a United States penal institution.
**Thirty-two years confinement and a fine of sixty-four
ounces of gold.**

I suggest that indictment and punishment for any repeat Class I
misdemeanor crime be assessed as a fourth-degree felony. Further,
for a second felony conviction, require a double sentence for the
crime last committed, with the exception of a second capital offense, which should remain at the maximum sentence of thirty-
two years. No third-offense category is needed. It is doubtful that
anyone will defy America's Man on Horseback three times.

CHAPTER SEVEN

Ending Crime, Riots, and Lawlessness
❦

Start your new prison system by abolishing federal prisons. Merge them with state prisons under the jurisdiction of the state where the federal facility is located. This allows prisoners from all socioeconomic levels to know one another and to share ideas. Integrating federal and state prison cultures lets every would-be federal or state lawbreaker know that any violation of your laws, whether white-collar or otherwise, is on a par with any other crime.

Convicted corporate chieftains and investment bankers have much in common with gang leaders; they differ only in methods. Should Hell not be crime-segregated, surely they will meet again. Do not fear commingling more intelligent federal prisoners with less-bright state convicts. The more sophisticated federal lawbreakers will not become trouble-making leaders of their more vicious state counterparts. Rather, they will use all their intellect and negotiating skills to keep their craniums uncracked and their rectums unbreached.

Arrange for criminals to serve their time in dishonor in a foreign land, since they refused to live in the United States with honor as law-abiding citizens. Remember that nineteenth-century England's crime began to wane only after accelerating shipments of convicts to overseas prisons. (The first batch of 730 convicts was transported to Australia in 1787; by 1830, 58,000 convicts had been shipped to Australia from English and Irish prisons.) Consider African countries to accommodate light-skinned American convicts and Siberia to accommodate criminals of darker pigmentation. (These countries, even at your time, have great needs for gold. Without doubt, they will house and feed your felons for one-half or less than American prisons cost.) Geography related to color will inhibit those prone to escape — color-coded criminals contrast nicely with local inhabitants. Families and friends of dark-skinned prisoners will send mail to and receive it from Siberia: Igarka, Magadan, and Vorkuta. Light-skinned convicts will correspond from exotic African paradises in Brazzaville, Kigali, Kinshasa, and Kisangani. Mail from chilly Kolyma and warm Mogadishu will signify the high status of odious prisoners. Do not discriminate by gender. Women's prisons are available in Africa, while camps at Balagannoye, Elgen, and Talon can be refurbished and opened quickly. Nor should you be concerned with temporary U.S. prison overcrowding. America's declaration of war against crime will solve this problem. For now, you are preparing the way before the battle begins.

Do not wait for new arrests, trials, and sentencing; activate the overseas flow of convicted criminals. Reduce the stateside prison population by 5 percent and reduce the number of prisons. National productivity is not associated with penitentiaries. American prisoner-watchers can be gainfully employed in the growth of food or the production of goods.

Allow each state to contribute 5 percent of its prison population to seed the overseas operation. Rest assured that state leaders will rid themselves of the most venomous troublemakers in their custody. Well-mannered convicts remaining in American prisons will become the rule, not the exception. But do not demand state participation. Instead, if a state fails to deliver 5 percent, cut off federal funding for prisons in that state. This should encourage conformity to your program, but if not, permit those states with leaders of a like mind as you to cover the shortfall of outgoing prisoners.

With the 5-percent relocation per year of America's hardest-to-manage convicts, coupled with your systemized new crime sentencing to overseas prisons, crime will be relegated to a meaningless and archaic throwback of an earlier, decadent America.

Along with these aggressive measures, however, your sympathy and mercy will be valued most by the pusillanimous portion of the populace should you do the following:

- Immediately send all prisoners on death row to Africa or Siberia and commute each sentence of execution to a new prison term of thirty-two years.
- Let gang members with matching pigmentation accompany each other to the same foreign prison.
- Enter into a custodial agreement with each foreign country to ensure that prison conditions and prisoner rights will not be less than those granted that country's incarcerated criminals.
- Do not enter into prison agreements with African nations that permit their citizens to eat chimpanzees. When chimpanzee and human diets are the same, the flesh of chimpanzees and humans tastes similar. There would be a danger that American convicts would be consumed as food.
- Give each overseas prisoner a written warning of the dangers of having mouth-to-penis and penis-to-rectum-to-prostate sex with guards and fellow inmates. Forewarn them that should they succumb to this practice and acquire *Slim*, they will never return to the United States. To stand fast and say no should be meaningful to criminals, since rapists of my time believed that rape was consensual because "no person can be raped unwillingly."
- Permit convicted attorneys to escape the color barrier — send the light-skinned to Siberia and the dark-skinned to Africa. They deserve special handling. (Further color-integration of other loathsome criminals, such as serial killers, may be in order. The negative reactions of other prisoners to their presence will offset the possibilities of escaping and color-blending with the local inhabitants.)

LAWYERS have not existed always. In older times, one presented one's case directly to the judge; but judges tended to rule in favor of the best orator, regardless of right or wrong. Lawyers emerged as understandable mouthpieces for the incomprehensible.

Law has never been the purest of professions, and antilawyer

sentiment has simmered for centuries. Since 1964, American lawyers, whether suing or defending, enriched themselves without
historical precedent, mastering their art and consuming America's productivity. Biblical stories about plagues of locusts pale in
comparison to the excessive grazing of attorneys. Attorneys are
parasites, sucking the financial blood from honest Americans.
Lawyers are feared more than ticks that transmit Lyme disease, af-
fixing themselves to the lifeblood of individuals and corporations
in greater numbers than ticks on a deer. Attorneys are so feared by
so many that they share the top rungs on the ladder of hate with
politicians. Crooked lawyer-politicians perch precariously on the
very highest rung.

In passing, I have heard some kind words for lawyers. Many
think very well of the few who teach in universities and well of
those who sit on the Supreme Court of the United States. Relatives
sometimes, though not always, think kindly of attorney kin. Perhaps the best that can be said of lawyers is that they collect no welfare for themselves.

You, America's Man on Horseback, need not dispose of lawyers
as advocated by Shakespeare's Dick the Butcher or made real by
Mao Tse-tung. Overseas incarceration can alleviate the burgeoning
bane of America — dishonest attorneys. It is now you who make
the laws determining what is honest and dishonest, not lawyers.

Consider doubling the sentences (but do not exceed the maximum of thirty-two years) for lawyers convicted of *any* crime committed while a member of the bar. This edict places a multitude of
nefarious attorneys on the horns of a dilemma. Should they quit
their practice, thus signaling fear that their crimes will be found
out? Or should they continue to practice believing that, in their arrogance, they can conceal their crimes from discovery and themselves from prosecution?

Little attention was given attorneys entering federal prisons,
which were not unlike country clubs; in contrast, much publicity
will surround the first lawyers sent to serve time in overseas prisons. Graphic news coverage will dramatize their high-status
demise and serve them up as examples to sober lawyers who,
then, should practice their profession honestly in a law-abiding,
principled, and perhaps less parasitic fashion. In addition, as the

number of lawyers will shrink when the new justice system is in place, excess attorneys could become salespeople and use their silver-tongued talents to sell the country's manufactured goods and farm products, thus benefiting the nation more in this manner than in their previous selling of strife.

Study the landscape for more bitter weeds, Mr. President. For example, include double sentences for public officeholders who commit *any* crimes while in office. One in five hundred Americans in my time holds public office. At your time, the percentage will undoubtedly worsen. Though you cannot make the dishonest honest, you can make dishonest, clever lawyers and officeholders think again when they consider fleecing the hardworking and the honest. And for those found out, convicted, and shipped overseas, you have given them time to think, period.

*　*　*　*

Your unorthodox treatment of crime and punishment will undoubtedly produce unforeseen side effects. One such quizzical twist I can predict and perhaps explain. Twelve months into your crime eradication program, the physiognomy of new criminals will begin to change. Their visages will have a common appearance: mean, malevolent, vicious, antisocial, tough. They will look hardened, older, and scragglier than those committing crimes before your criminal agenda. The answer lies in the drastic drop in criminal activity, thus the small number of criminals who share a common countenance. More importantly, attractive young men, regardless of ethnicity, will pursue other activities than crime, for they realize that their youth and pleasing appearance would attract too many sexual advances in African and Siberian prisons.

*　*　*　*

Think through your crime-stopping agenda to foresee flaws and eliminate time-consuming restructuring. Monitoring and maintenance are necessary, but continual changes weaken any program's effectiveness.

Anticipate criminal escapes from overseas prisons. Escapees mock American justice. Deal severely with them. Rather than advancing gold to build more secure foreign prisons, make it nearly impossible for escaped prisoners to flee successfully. Simple methods bring quicker results than complicated ones. A bounty in gold, one equal to the cost of maintaining the fugitive for the remainder of his term, could be offered as an incentive for the return of the remains of an escapee. For instance, if the sentence is sixteen years and the escape is made in year two, a sum equal to fourteen years' cost-of-confinement could be offered for proof that the escaped prisoner has ceased to exist (in this case about 250 gold ounces). If the bounty is unclaimed upon the first anniversary of the escape, double it. Should this not provide the desired result during year two, then double it again for year three, and remain at that bounty until collected. No one, regardless of cunning or wealth, can hide for long anywhere in the world without help. Someone, somewhere, will know of the escapee's location. The amount of reward, with worldwide publicity, will spawn a new industry — international bounty hunting.

Declare escaped criminals outside the protection of American law. In time, such outside-the-law escapees will not be safe in any country, even those that harbor terrorists, for the love of money turns many a head. As criminals relentlessly pursued their victims, so should outlaws be hunted down. Anticipate all sorts of proof of demise — heads, hands, feet, and even whole pickled bodies. Set standards of uniform proof, as some would sell body parts more than once. Pay promptly and anonymously; records of delivery of the reward and taxes on such payments are not necessary. Further, charge any American aiding, abetting, or harboring an escaped convict with a felony. If found guilty, the individual or group must complete the escapee's unserved time.

Of course, your policy will be abused. Since escape is the prerequisite to reward, some overseas prisoners will be tricked into flight. Greedy guards may coerce criminals to abandon the safety of the prison. The hazard of being kidnapped for bounty will keep those criminals with longer sentences continually on guard. (In good conscience, you must acquaint overseas prisoners of the protective benefits within the prison. Advise them of their certain fatality should they abandon their prison home and move outside the protection of American law. Even when unheeded, make the effort.) Some fugitives caught by bounty hunters in the first year will be fed in secret, and their fresh remains delivered the second year when the reward doubles. But have your agents pay regardless of circumstances; you are a man of your word and are above quibbling.

You now have the infrastructure to prevent future crime in America. Resolving the country's financial disorder must wait; of more immediacy is your decisive and swift action to resolve the lawlessness sapping our nation's strength. It is of no account that some folk heroes may spring temporarily from those who defy you, particularly those you oblige to make an early payment of their debt to nature. However, few songs will be written and sung about their misdeeds.

Now you must confront the cavernous abscess that began as a pimple in 1964. Now is the time for you, America's commander in chief, to declare war on domestic terrorism, national riots, armed warfare, organized crime, gangs, land pirates, and ochlocracy. Expect crime families, rioters, predatory gangs, and sellers of illegal drugs to force open warfare. Let the country see you when your blood is up.

Rioters and looters, though armed and dangerous, can be liquidated handily. Expect a larger firefight when gangs, meaner and more numerous than rioters, are rooted from their hiding places. Sellers of illegal drugs, prison escapees, parole violators, members of organized crime, and bail jumpers will take longer to locate. They, too, will fight like cornered rats when found. The easiest to find and the most indignant will be overconfident drug lords and the heads of organized crime families long kept free by bribes and lawyers. The most surprised when they realize how soon they are to appear before their maker will be murderers and rapists, previously freed by court technicalities, shyster lawyers, or unjust, sympathetic juries. Give no quarter.

While you have an established position against the death penalty for criminal actions, remember Machiavelli's words: "when many suffer, few seek for revenge, because universal injuries are borne with greater patience than particular ones," and "a thing done is ended." Ensure that the upcoming carnage occurs just once, even though you will not be able to eradicate all those deserving. Repetitive liquidations are costly, time consuming, and unnecessary and are only an option for those who take pleasure in riding the black horse. You do not.

The American public dislikes reading about, hearing of, or viewing mass elimination of their fellow Americans. You cannot benefit from television, radio, or newspaper accounts of such operations, regardless of how flatteringly they would portray you. Therefore, allow a select government agency to provide a minimum number of vague news releases.

Give early warning of the impending doom for rioters, gangs, and criminals. Then, place the Marine Commandant in charge of America's cleansing. The United States Marine Corps, being the world's finest military arm, would expect to take the point. During this dire discharge of duty, mobilize all others — including the Federal Bureau of Investigation, the Air Force, Army, Navy, and related state agencies — under the Commandant. In a short time, thousands of murderous Americans and felonious illegal aliens will cease to exist.

Take a lesson from the citrus farmers, who, after a hard freeze, rid their trees of deadwood to enable them to grow and reproduce. They know that in order to remove all the deadwood, some living wood must be pruned. Similarly, surgeons excising cancerous growths concern themselves less with removing some healthy body tissue and more with having "got it all." And so it must be with you.

Close all educational facilities, financial institutions, and nonessential functions until hostilities cease. Provide armed escorts for firemen and hospital and power plant workers. Warn law-abiding citizens to stay inside, lock their doors, and not venture outside. Realize that many curious, though innocent, citizens will be caught up in the cleansing. Concentrations of rioters, looters, gangs, land pirates, and lawbreakers of all kinds guarantee that stray missiles, from both friendly and facinorous sources, will strike the innocent along with the guilty.

Take bold action to protect innocent Hispanics, Negroes, Orientals, and other minorities from thugs among them and from angry Caucasian mobs. Feed, clothe, and provide shelter away from the slums for those without criminal records, for those who want to be a part of your new America.

The few criminals inadvertently taken alive will offer up the names of those who initially escape the military net. While none look forward to an African or Siberian prison, these informants will be grateful to respire. Do not waste time or gold on burned-out slums. Crimes are committed most often where criminals feel comfortable. There is no reason to provide new buildings for those with a bent toward arson. Let burned buildings remain as monuments to a decadent America that deemed it politically correct to foul your nest and acquire a new one via a government handout.

The armed forces monitor closely how you judge those under military command who fail to execute orders. How do you deal with compassionate soldiers and law enforcers who lay down their arms rather than fire on fellow Americans? Determine guilt quickly and hang the mutineers in front of your troops with neither apology nor fanfare.

In a matter of days you will have ended America's organized crime, homegrown terrorism, riots, gang warfare, and ethnic slaughter. Congratulations pour in from Americans pleased with your swift, successful course of action. Open dissent to your policies is muted temporarily. The thoughtful among your opposition begin to think not about how they can offend you but how they must become your friend. But you have only fulfilled your promise to America, and, as Machiavelli advised, "You must always have understood that things done out of necessity neither should nor can merit praise or blame."

Hail to America's Man on Horseback!

CHAPTER EIGHT

Domestic Law Enforcement

Justice will come again to the nation, although an admittedly harsher justice. Perilous times will make it so. American law enforcement officers will support your cause more than they supported that of any previous president.

Unquestionably you need the backing of American peace officers as well as their enthusiasm and unqualified support in order to enforce your agenda. But with this also comes baggage accumulated over a half-century. Five decades of escalating crime lured many peace officers to participate in lucrative criminal activities. As crime diminishes, rather than righting wrongs, too many constables, police, sheriffs, undersheriffs, and federal law enforcement officers will go back to old habits and begin to wrong the right. Exact the same punishment for law officers who break the law as for any other person who commits a crime.

Once major crime is vanquished, domestic law enforcement could become your Achilles' heel. As the honest public loses its fear of crime, second thoughts about your presidency will surface. You will be vulnerable to criticism about corrupt, power-hungry crime fighters. While not ignoring such charges, do not become enmeshed in ferreting out lawbreakers among close-mouthed law enforcement groups. You will need to simplify the removal of dishonest law enforcement officers and the promotion of honest ones.

More than a few big-city police forces have been notoriously corrupt, some going back to the nineteenth century. Even sheriffs and police in sparsely populated counties and small towns have been known periodically to head large-scale criminal activities. Expect the majority of American law officers to be honest, however, since law enforcement was considered honorable employment from America's inception to 1964. Because of high standards for employment, the highest percentages of honest versus dishonest are in the Federal Bureau of Investigation and the Secret Service. The largest numbers of dishonest police will be among those employed in corrupt-from-the-top-down departments in major cities, since those officers taking bribes from criminals, a felony offense, were rarely prosecuted.

During your Marine-led assault on crime, all law enforcement officers were inducted temporarily into America's armed forces and participated in open warfare during that brief period of cleansing. Even though they fought successfully in combat, do not permit death squads to deal with your enemies now. Neither should you dampen the enthusiasm of law officers nor hobble their efforts by keeping them in too tight a halter. In chaotic times, which you still face, heavy-handed interrogation is not the same as death squads. Misconduct on your behalf is the prerequisite for you to forgive mistakes made by law officers; it is important to judge the degree of error. Remember: You need American law officers and they need you.

To simplify dealing with domestic law enforcement, I suggest a statement similar to the following for current law enforcement officers to sign at once, new officers upon enlistment and all officers annually thereafter. The Internal Revenue Service can best review and oversee investigation of the executed documents.

This legal document will bring about immediate, midrange, and long-range results. First, and perhaps most important, a sizable number of law officers will resign or retire early rather than sign this affidavit. Let them go in peace. Do not offer amnesty or initiate criminal hunts. Any past crime that surfaces later can be handled as a matter of course.

Midrange results involve current law officers, those who have committed felony crimes or who have knowledge of undisclosed

[TABLE 6]

Statement of Disclosure of Criminal Activities

It is the legal responsibility of the Internal Revenue Service to oversee the United States domestic law enforcement agencies. To create new ethical standards of conduct, the Internal Revenue Service developed this questionnaire to cleanse the country of all federal, state, county, and municipal law enforcement officers who have violated the law or who have been passive observers as the law was violated.

Answer the following questions regarding your conduct beginning with the first day you became a law enforcement officer to the current date.

All the information reflected in this statement will be held in confidence by the Internal Revenue Service.

Warning: An untrue statement, either answer or explanation, will result in an indictment with a minimum charge of a fourth-degree felony. The statute of limitations for such indictments shall extend to the date of death of the declarant whose name is shown below.

Declarant Name (print)	Social Security No.
First Law Enforcement Employer	Date Employment Began
Current Law Enforcement Employer	Date Employment Began

Any *yes* answer to the following questions, including any mitigating circumstances, must be explained in detail below or on an additional attachment.

1. Have you been either indicted or convicted of a criminal proceeding, or are you a named subject of a pending criminal proceeding?
   [ ] yes   [ ] no
2. Have you committed any felony crime?
   [ ] yes   [ ] no
3. Do you have knowledge of any felony crime having been committed by someone whom you know that is not already formally on record as part of a criminal investigation?
   [ ] yes   [ ] no

Explanation required for *yes* answer to question 1:

_____

_____

Explanation required for _yes_ answer to question 2:

_____
_____
_____
_____
_____
_____

Explanation required for _yes_ answer to question 3:

_____
_____
_____
_____
_____
_____

Declarant Signature: _____
Date: _____

On the above date, the foregoing statement was signed by Declarant. We sign our names as witnesses.

_____
Witness Signature

_____
Witness Name (printed)

_____
Witness Signature

_____
Witness Name (printed)

felonious activities. It is this last item that will trouble many law officers. Some, though honest themselves, know of corrupt officers, perhaps even a superior. The timorous and the imprudent will resign rather than denounce another — an effective means of ridding the ranks of the faint-hearted and the foolish. Treat the passive observers who know, but swear that they do not know, the same as those who commit crimes. In addition to the fourth-degree felony for an untrue statement by the declarant, indict and prosecute both the observer and the found-out criminal for whatever crime occurred.

The most lasting outcome of this program will be your implicit trust of the domestic law enforcement agencies. In turn, these agents must trust you, Mr. President; your actions must show them that you support their endeavors on your behalf. America's law officers will join with you to eliminate the professional criminals who, in the past, rarely failed to overwhelm honest, hard-working Americans.

Quarantine

❧

Health is a continuing property measurable by the
individual's ability to rally from insults, whether chemical,
physical, infectious, psychological or social.

J. RALPH AUDY

You addressed a number of chemical, physical, and psychological insults to individuals with your anticrime agenda. And when you rebuild the American work ethic, you will remedy a social insult afflicting many Americans since 1964. Consider now attending to one infectious insult: *Slim,* caused by the invasion of the Human Immunodeficiency Virus, which in all probability is prevalent at your time.

As living organisms, bacteria and viruses seek always to advance themselves. In my time, there are about twenty-five thousand named diseases of humans and cures for some five thousand of them. Even though medical advances slow and even eradicate a few of history's most virulent infections, new diseases as well as mutated old maladies will continue to afflict humanity until human beings are no more.

The following quotes are excerpted from William H. McNeill's *Plagues and Peoples* (1976) published years before the existence of *Slim* was recognized worldwide.

> Disease-producing parasites were quite as successful as people
> in taking advantage of new opportunities for occupying novel
> ecological niches that opened up as a result of human actions
> that distorted natural patterns of plant and animal distribution.

71

... [T]he fate of rabbits in Australia when exposed to an exceedingly virulent new infection may be used to illustrate the manner in which a virus infection acts when it penetrates a new population and then survives to become endemic.

... Human efforts to reduce the number of rabbits in Australia took a new turn in 1950 when the virus of myxomatosis (a distant relative of human smallpox) was successfully transferred to the rabbit population of that continent. The initial impact was explosive: in a single season an area as great as all of western Europe was infected. The death rate among rabbits that got the disease in the first year was 99.8 per cent. In the next year, however, the death rate went down to a mere 90 per cent; seven years later mortality among infected rabbits was only 25 per cent. Obviously, very rigorous and rapid selection had occurred among rabbits and among viral strains as well. Samples of the virus derived from wild rabbits became measurably milder in virulence with each successive year.

Whether or not a new disease begins as lethally as myxomatosis did, the process of mutual accommodation between host and parasite is fundamentally the same. A stable new disease pattern can arise only when both parties manage to survive their initial encounter and, by suitable biological and cultural adjustments, arrive at a mutually tolerable arrangement. In all such processes of adjustment bacteria and viruses have the advantage of a much shorter time between generations. . . . [H]istorical experience of later ages suggests that something like 120 to 150 years are needed for human populations to stabilize their response to drastic new infections.

... Given the brevity of rabbit generations — observed as six to ten months from birth to parenthood in Australia — this three-year span was equivalent to 90 to 150 years on a human scale, if we calculate a human generation to be 25 years. In other words, comparable generational time may be needed for humans and for rabbits to adjust to an initially lethal new disease.

... [T]he period required for medieval European populations to absorb the shock of renewed exposure to [the bubonic] plague seems to have been between 100 and 133 years, i.e.,

about five to six human generations. This closely parallels the
time Amerindian and Pacific island populations later needed to
make an even more drastic adjustment to altered epidemiologi-
cal conditions and suggests that, as in the case of Australian rabbits exposed to myxomatosis, 1950–53, there are natural
rhythms at work that limit and define the demographic consequences of sudden exposure to initially very lethal infections.

. . . [F]or a new ecological niche, wherever presented, tends
to be occupied quickly by whatever organism — human or non-
human — thereby multiplies its kind.

. . . *Infectious bacterial and viral diseases that pass directly from
human to human with no intermediate host are therefore the diseases of
civilization par excellence.* [Emphasis added.]

. . . Sometimes new infections actually manifest their greatest
virulence among young adults, owing, some doctors believe, to
excessive vigor of this age-group's antibody reactions to the in-
vading disease organism. Population losses within the twenty-
to-forty age bracket are obviously far more damaging to society
at large than comparably numerous destruction of either the
very young or the very old.

. . . The quarantine rules which became general in Christian
ports of the Mediterranean in the sixteenth century were therefore well founded.

Politicians and leading scientists at no time disputed McNeill's
assertions, yet they never informed the public of the import of this
knowledge to their daily lives. People were never told by government officials or medical practitioners that *Slim* would probably
destroy Americans for five to six generations. After first denying
that the disease existed, they later led the public to believe that a
cure was right around the corner. Media attention focused on a
cure and life-extending drugs for the afflicted rather than on eliminating the spread of *Slim*. Much ado was made about those infected with the virus who did not develop *Slim*, although McNeill's
rabbit-to-human generations anticipated that a virus such as *Slim*
would spare 20 per 100,000 infected humans between the years
1980 and 2017, 10,000 per 100,000 between 2018 and 2054, and
25,000 per 100,000 between 2055 and 2091.

The tenth-generation scientific research community in the United States had no world peers. Federal funding exploded to seek a cure: money came from deficit spending and from rerouting research monies from such other catastrophic illnesses as cancer and heart disease. Backed by this unprecedented amount of federal spending for a single disease, the nation's most impressive scientists concentrated on a cure for *Slim*. Knowledgeable, but easily intimidated, politicians from the same tenth generation allowed *Slim* to kill hemophiliacs and other innocents through contaminated blood supplies and inadvertent infections rather than invoke quarantine.

America was misled, Mr. President. Citizens were not given a choice between a possible 125-year plague or containment by quarantine. After the realization of *Slim*'s epidemic propensities, the word *quarantine* was avoided; it became an epithet without equal to homosexuals in America. Further, Congress enacted federal laws to prevent the dissemination of blood test results identifying the carriers of *Slim*. *Slim* privacy was paramount.

M E N and women with homosexual preferences are among the most industrious and productive members of any civilization. Not rooted in genes, homosexuality stems from child-rearing practices, primarily those of dominant mothers.

Freedom from behavioral restraints, instant gratification, and blatant homosexuality are part and parcel of the final two generations in each of history's ten-generation epochs, the Age of Decadence. Ancient Greece and Rome are two among many examples, and love between men flourished as a respected Japanese subculture during the fifty years prior to 1868.

Penis-to-rectum-to-prostate sex produced the highest ratios of those acquiring *Slim*. The sharing of contaminated needles among illegal drug users took second place. A sizable number of needle-sharers were members of America's derelict destitute. This wretched collection of men and women, referred to as "homeless," was fawned over by the media and politicians alike. Good-hearted citizens gave these vagrants food, clothing, and money, much of which was spent on alcohol and illegal drugs, thus perpetuating the cycle.

Unwritten laws were sanctioned on their behalf. In many cities, drifters urinated, defecated, and slept on public sidewalks, and vagrants could curse and accost and expose their genitals to passersby. These actions became idiosyncratic "rights" for the homeless. Some city governments attacked the problem by requiring business owners to clean public areas adjacent to their property of the feces and other litter left by the homeless.

In America's largest cities, *Slim* was rampant among the homeless. Politicians decided that the prevention of *Slim* among the hopeless merited government intervention. Federal and state money paid for booklets describing the danger of acquiring *Slim* through shared needles. Derelicts received new needles and syringes in return for used ones. "Watchers" were employed to make periodic checks to ensure that illegal drugs were injected using new needles and syringes, without sharing. This work involved administration, supervision, salaries, and related costs.

Sex among the homeless also engaged the attention of politicians, since more people still acquired *Slim* through copulation than through drug use. Condoms joined booklets and new needles and syringes as free aids distributed to prevent *Slim*. Watchers could watch but not act when members of this sad group coupled. Sometimes condoms were used, sometimes not. As many homeless copulated while dazed from drugs or alcohol, a condom, if used, often was affixed haphazardly or came off entirely.

Politicians held discussions to address the "condom problem." The assignment of "minders," one to each homeless person, was advocated. Minders were first popularized in England, where they are assigned, one per unmanageable student, to alleviate behavioral problems in the national education system. As each homeless person would have a personal minder at all times to mind his behavior, watchers would no longer be needed, or so went the logic. Minders could be hired from the ranks of those on welfare, converting them to workfare. This could provide jobs for three people, each working an eight-hour shift per derelict. However, the political fear that former welfare recipients might contract *Slim* from the homeless was enough to place that political plum on hold.

Close to the end of each civilization's ten-generation cycle, homosexuals are persecuted, as are other nonconformist minorities, usually the extremes of those most successful and those least industrious. The maiming and killing of homosexuals and the homeless in the early twenty-first century were fragments of the rabid violent crime that you inherited and ended.

At the time of your presidency, the general population will be solidly against growth in the ranks of the homeless and the practice of homosexuality. Homosexuals, both men and women, will no longer be a dominant force in American society. Beginning with your presidency and for the next eight generations, most homosexuals will retreat to the closet of marriage and procreation. But their legacy, *Slim*, will remain.

Determine the carriers of *Slim* through nationwide blood testing. Then invoke quarantine. Testing will surface myriad other maladies, from diabetes to sexually transmitted diseases, many of which can be treated immediately and successfully. Use this information to establish a permanent DNA file for each American. This data may be helpful when new or mutated bacteria and viruses find contemporary niches in American bodies. Implementation, follow-through, and quarantine decisions can be administered by the Internal Revenue Service. Make this agency the repository of America's DNA file. The health of the citizenry may benefit from, and you will find a multitude of other uses for, such a computerized file.

Two quarantine locations are sufficient: one for behavior-caused *Slim* and one for all others. Contain *Slim* by periodically retesting all individuals in America at six-month intervals, thus saving numerous lives. Provide compassionate accommodation and professional, life-extending treatment for all the afflicted. Quarantine will control America's problem. (Since *Slim* could be a serious problem outside the United States, encourage nongovernment, private, charitable funding for American scientists searching for a cure.)

Mr. President, thoughts of quarantine to contain *Slim* are in the minds of many citizens in my time but are never given voice. Every current member of the U.S. House of Representatives and the U.S. Senate along with the president of the United States dread the homosexual community's wrath regarding quarantine more than they fear *Slim* itself. Not you.

Reestablishing the American Work Ethic

❧

How awful the American economy must be at your ascendancy! I can only speculate about the combined percentage of unemployed and underemployed Americans. One in four? One in three? Worse? What term do the politicians at your time use for the economic wreckage they have wrought? On what or whom do they place the blame?

I know that political profligacy brought about hyperinflation and worthless currency. The time of reckoning came when off-budget expenditures, government loan guarantees, benevolent bestowing, and outright theft by lawmakers and their friends could no longer be covered by tax increases and the sale of government bonds. It took eight generations for Americans to amass the wealth that the following two generations squandered.

That a person of your caliber is president makes plain that the economy of the United States is near the bottom. Therefore the rise is equally near, as nothing worthwhile stays down for long. But it is improbable that America can regain world economic supremacy in your thirty-year presidency unless you use the military for conquest. Conquest can produce economic superiority in less than a generation, but withhold that action for now.

To revitalize the economy, the American work ethic must be reinstilled in the population. End government support for those unwilling to do their work well and for those who refuse to work at all. Ensure that all who want to work will be able to do so. Encourage productivity and competition in business.

When you repealed every federal, state, and local bill and statute that became law from 1964 on, you eliminated the American dole, effectively halting illegal immigration. (After 1964, most illegal aliens came to the United States to work at jobs rejected by those surfeited with government handouts.) Vast numbers of people were added to the labor force when welfare to able-bodied Americans ended. Eliminating mass crime, which sapped America's vitality, gave pause to millions of would-be felons; all but the most foolish seek gainful employment over criminal activity. Additionally, the repeal of all laws since 1964 rid the nation of federal costs associated with employing useless bureaucratic slugs. Former bureaucrats seeking jobs that match their competence benefit those employing unskilled or lackey labor. More important, the absence of bureaucracy encourages entrepreneurs to start new businesses.

Now eliminate civil service. Avoid the corruption and incompetence associated with government employment by establishing rigid hiring practices and allowing supervisors to fire "with cause." Add to your criminal-penalty list any attempted use of political patronage in hiring decisions. It is better to stop political hiring than to suffer the incompetence of civil service employees who cannot be fired. Competition for jobs will be as keen as competition for customers.

Eliminate government-mandated unemployment payments to terminated or laid-off employees, public or private. The more industrious and frugal will accrue savings for such an event and find new employment. (Some employees provoke termination as a means of vacationing until unemployment benefits run out.) Corporations of my time would gladly have paid 3 percent of their pretax profits in additional taxes to rid themselves of unemployment compensation expenses. Most important, employees will work harder and become more productive in order to retain their jobs.

The nation's infrastructure is in decay in my time, certainly rotten in yours. Now that both the federal government and private industry can fire "with cause" and without governmental intervention, make the federal government the employer of last resort; guarantee manual-labor employment for every citizen. (When necessary, provide dormitories for these government-employed manual laborers and child-care facilities for their children.) Expect this to be a temporary measure, as was President Franklin Roosevelt's action almost a century before your ascendancy, when, during the Great Depression of the 1930s, radical federal work programs provided employment for many Americans. The Works Project Administration made few demands for excellence in employee performance, while the Civilian Conservation Corps developed high-spirited teamwork among its hardworking employees. Although results differed among the many methods used to provide gainful employment, the overall results were successful: people had jobs and the dignity that work provides.

Guaranteed federal employment coupled with termination "with cause" by government supervisors provides at best sustenance for those needing a job and at worst a weeding-out way station. It will force those who give lip service to wanting work but who do not work into finding some private individual or charity to support them.

Much can be accomplished with the initial surge in federal employment of the needy. Besides repairing nuclear power plants, bridges, highways, dams, water and sewer works, set them to constructing single-family homes for the elderly poor in rural sections of America, providing space for gardens and livestock so that they can maintain their self-respect and contribute to their food requirements. Make caring for the nation's honest elderly one hallmark of America's new beginning. Stipulate only that all recipients have never committed a felony. It is not fitting to reward society's older criminals by allowing them to mingle with those who led crime-free lives.

*   *   *   *

Do not repair Washington, D.C. Consider copying Japan's shogunate "tent headquarters" originated by Minamoto Yoritomo in 1192 and resurrected by Tokugawa Ieyasu in 1600. Relocate your supreme center of operations. Divorce the diseased District of Columbia. Remove yourself, the host, from the now unemployed, swarming parasites — loathsome lobbyists, unproductive federal employees, and welfare recipients. Without federal access for lobbyists, employment for the near-worthless, and funds for welfare, Washington, D.C., will be abandoned. Allow weather, decay, and fires to destroy the city and its surrounding suburbs. Employ the military to protect only American shrines, anticipating a triumphant return. In time, Mr. President, raze everything except the great monuments to America's past glories, then rebuild the nation's capital around them to reflect the new splendor of the American Empire.

*   *   *   *

Six generations ago, in *Democracy in America*, Alexis de Tocqueville wrote about the uniqueness of American bankruptcy: "There is no American legislation against fraudulent bankruptcies. Is it because there are no bankrupts? No, on the contrary, it is because there are so many. In the mind of the majority the fear of being prosecuted as a bankrupt is greater than the apprehension of being ruined by other bankrupts, so the public conscience has a sort of guilty tolerance for an offense which everyone individually condemns."

Tocqueville would not recognize the United States at my time. Not a single American feared bankruptcy prosecution, while the majority were apprehensive of being ruined by the bankruptcies of others. Few if any of those damaged would question that contemporary bankruptcy laws, written by lawyers, increasingly enriched debtors and lawyers to the detriment of legitimate complainants and lenders. Legal "insolvency" and legal "abdication" of wrongful acts made many rich and wronged countless Americans. Current bankruptcy laws mock the work ethic; bankruptcy scams spread as a plague.

Only you can end the injustice that robs Americans of just repayment of loans and just reparations for widespread maleficence. Only you can bring order to bankruptcy disorder, something American leaders before you lacked the courage and resolve to do. Of course you could outlaw bankruptcies altogether, even resurrect old English debtor laws entailing imprisonment, or perhaps something altogether new. Consider rescinding the right to vote and to hold public office for bankruptcy filers — corporate directors, corporate officers, individual bankrupts — and the attorneys representing them. Inevitably, many among the honest and the dishonest bankrupts will secure new debt. The dishonest will again commit wrongs, lawyers will prosper, and citizens will be damaged. However, without the right to vote or hold office and without your blessing, the number of Americans harmed by bankruptcy fraud will be reduced.

Your casting out of all laws since 1964 loosened the many shackles binding manufacturing and trade and fueled entrepreneurship. Should a government-mandated minimum wage still exist, eliminate this financial farce as a keystone of your economic policy. Equality has never really existed in the workplace or in paychecks. With unregulated free enterprise, the marketplace sets employee pay. During your presidency, Americans will rediscover an earlier American belief: a day's work for a day's pay. America will adjust to a return to its early-twentieth-century work ethic, although perhaps not as quickly as it fell into decadence.

Cast out every law that stands in the way of an American work ethic. Adopt a "leave it alone" policy for business. Allow productivity to soar. The businessman's love of money is an evil, but for now your best option is to encourage the matchless abilities of entrepreneurs to sire companies and beget meaningful employment. Rapaciousness and worker exploitation will come, but private-sector jobs are lesser evils than out-of-work despair or lower-paying last-resort government employment. You will need new criminal laws to hold in check dishonest business predators without killing the benefits of competitive industry. Permit workers to organize and honor their strikes without interference. You will be able to correct business abuses in the future, when you have more time.

Combine the competitive way of life that existed in the 1900s with the technology of your time. Encourage the acquisition of money, inspire competition. But do not embrace all the values of that time. For instance, in sawmills of the day it was preferable to have a man die on the job rather than a mule: another man, so went the logic, could be hired, but a mule had to be bought. Avoid such cavalier disregard for human life. Consider reinstating some of the more practical health and safety laws. And do not give employers the legal right to fire employees without cause. "At will" termination destroys the spirit of honest, industrious, and competitive employees while, at the same time, it unjustly rewards sycophants, toadies, and rectum-kissers. After all, America's strength lies in its hardworking people.

Despite these changes, the favorable ratio of American achievers to nonachievers will not equal those of the 1900s. A large number of the children of the ninth and tenth generations were born to shop, not reared to work. With whatever ratios that exist, America will still have enough entrepreneurs to plant and grow companies and to create new jobs.

Do not listen to those who say that things *and* people are different today. Regardless of the technological marvels that mankind has at your time, or the world position America occupies in manufacturing and marketing, the nature of man has not changed since written history began. People are the same — good, bad, and all degrees between. Ensure equal opportunity for all Americans, but do not concern yourself with creating equality. All men are not equal — mentally or physically. Equality between the simple and the clever, the weak and the strong, is as unnatural among humans as it is among the lower animals. Your task in restoring the United States to greatness does not lie in creating false equality among its citizens.

You brought corrupt legislators to heel and ended pork-barrel legislation, which solved one part of the spending problem. Refrain, however, from tinkering with money or business, either helping or hindering. No matter how well intended, when government intervenes, the value of currency and industry and the well-being of the nation's citizens suffer. No counsel is needed now about the merit of a gold standard to provide Americans with monetary stability. You will find that the government's vaults of gold are either hypothecated or empty, and much time will lapse before government gold coffers are refilled.

Once Americans are at work in productive endeavors, few nondominant immigrants will arrive to pick over dry bones. Still, various countries continue to punish their dominant moneymakers with adversarial laws and regulations and high taxes, much as America did prior to your ascendancy. Encourage, even solicit, the immigration of the oppressed, dominant minority of other countries. During the 1950s, many such people moved from England to the United States, helping our country and creating a "brain drain" in theirs. Later, dominant Cubans, Chinese, and Vietnamese who were shunned in their countries became immensely successful here. Dominant individuals such as these will not only better themselves but will deliver beneficial results to the United States.

Each and every citizen has a stake in the country and an obligation to pay for the government. Identify and tax every American, even the lowest paid. No more than three tax rates are needed — a 1-percent tax on the yearly income of the poorest 25 percent of individuals, a 20-percent annual income tax on the wealthiest 25 percent of citizens, and a 10-percent per annum tax on the remaining 50 percent of American income earners. Allow no deductions. Such a three-tiered tax rate will create a monetary surplus for any well-run country. Consider similar tax assessments for American corporations and start taxing all foundations, charitable or otherwise, at corporate rates. States that follow your federal cost-cutting examples will have no need for income taxes and only moderate requirements for sales taxes.

The Internal Revenue Service will be around at your time, though perhaps known by another name. With such simple tax returns coupled with little tax evasion because of your no-nonsense crime agenda, the agency's employee complement could be reduced, with those remaining being of the highest quality. But resist the urge to further cut the ranks of this agency, Mr. President; you need their eyes and ears to monitor citizen compliance in other areas. One such duty for the Internal Revenue Service could be a written accounting of all citizens. Just as the Normans had their Domesday Book in 1086, so should you.

*   *   *   *

Artifacts used in games of chance evidence that humans have gambled for millennia. Since written history and probably earlier — certainly since 3500 B.C., and perhaps for as long as forty thousand years — human nature has been allied with betting. Culture determines the method of betting, whether based on the outcome of strategy or physical skill or games of chance. While empires have been built by gambling on the outcome of conquest, funds derived from legalized gambling have never built a great nation. Abolish all forms of state-sanctioned betting, as work and luck are contradictions. Legalizing gambling is a nation's final act in dismembering the work ethic.

When you set aside all laws enacted since 1964, you eliminated legal gambling by lot — lotteries. The first modern sweepstakes were held by the state of New Hampshire in 1964. After that, to 1998, lotteries became a nationwide mania. Most, but not all, legalized casino gambling disappeared when you revoked the laws from 1964 on (casino gambling was legal in one state before 1964). In addition, a number of gambling industries such as horse and dog racing were also legal entities before then. Close them.

Do not permit debate on the issue of stopping state-sanctioned betting. Debate could polarize Americans more than any other issue. If you elect to stop all forms of legalized betting, the quicker you take action, the better the results. The question is not whether state-sanctioned gaming is good or evil, only whether you want it around.

Regardless of punishment, however, personal betting will prevail. Ignore it. You have nothing to gain by assessing severe penalties against Americans who bet with each other individually. Organized criminal gambling operations are another matter. Your crime enforcement placed these lawbreakers in overseas prisons to reside with bona fide losers.

If legalized gambling disappears at your direction, expect large-scale dissension from those with vested interests in the gambling industry. Be prepared for an onslaught of unfavorable publicity. People remember for a lifetime if property, money, or goods are taken from them. However, those unaffected pay little attention to what is taken from others. In this instance, all those suffering direct financial loss are gamblers by nature and by trade, otherwise they would not have invested their time and money in gaming ventures. Real gamblers, while expecting to win most of the time, know they will lose sometimes. Therefore, any gamblers who agitate against you are not true gamblers. They are fools. Treat them as such.

*   *   *   *

The American Empire's first generation faces the same problems as the Republic's first generation — food and shelter for its citizenry. Treat family-owned farms with the utmost respect and encourage the establishment of new ones. Limit the total tax on these farms to no more than 15 percent of their yield of grain, produce, dairy products, or livestock. Corporate agricultural businesses need little encouragement; tax them the same as other corporate enterprises. Convert vacant farmland to productive use by rewarding the most successful family-owned farms with more land. Let these farmers become wealthy as they feed America. See to it that those who are neither resourceful nor profitable seek other employment. Do not waste the land.

As you look over the decayed and profligate America of your inauguration, realize that your vision can surpass the best of the past of this splendid country. Reestablishing the work ethic in an economically devastated country requires hardships, but no more than those endured initially in building the nation. And such hardships pale in comparison to the suffering caused by the fiscal crisis and physical violence prevalent when your presidency began.

CHAPTER ELEVEN

Inheritance

✣

Taxing inherited wealth stands to be a thornier issue for you than it was for the lawmakers of my time. Be wary of trying to remedy the tenth generation's dissipation of inherited wealth through radical taxation of inheritances.

Class systems are designed to preserve individual family fortunes — money, goods, position, power, or the ownership of lands, minerals, or commerce. Each system has its roots in the dominance (achieving) trait as exhibited by the successes of its men. Unless the system limits marriages of its members to others within the upper class, family fortunes can erode and disappear within two generations.

Class systems perpetuate family fortunes for years — although not totally within the confines of the male lineage in every generation — by marriages between its families. In a closed system, marriages combining given numbers of dominant and nondominant (nonachieving) members of families within the class preserve family fortunes. The process reverses itself, nondominant to dominant and dominant to nondominant unions, in each subsequent generation.

This means that a family fortune is not totally at risk of being lost by a nondominant son. He most likely will marry a dominant daughter of another family in the approved class, thereby providing wealth or its equivalent from both sides of the marriage. In the next generation, then, dominant sons of that union may increase the combined family wealth. This system perpetuates the transmission and growth of fortunes.

Marriages within the class system that existed in England during the 1800s preserved it to a point. Some families in the upper class were of the dominant wife/nondominant husband combination. The nondominant husband rarely achieved notable success, a detail usually overlooked in the family's history. Also ignored was the wife's role, she being a mere female: owing to the wife's dominance, the children were probably dominant and successful, especially the firstborn male.

In the same generation, time period, and class, the opposite circumstance will have occurred in other families in which there was a dominant husband and nondominant wife. The husband achieved outstanding success, duly noted in the family chronicles. The wife, again because she was a woman rather than because of her lower dominance level, usually was not mentioned. The children, nondominant because of their mother, probably were unsuccessful.

Examining a succession of marriages, one most often sees dominance paired with nondominance. Dominant men increased the wealth, land, and power or preserved them for future dominant men. In addition, there were some sequential generations of dominant males, for example, when a dominant man married a dominant woman and produced a son who was dominant because of his mother. In these families the chance for success was favorably skewed for two consecutive generations.

If the birth rate of dominant children equals or exceeds that of nondominant children, the class can continue indefinitely.

A deterioration of control by an upper class, in England in the 1800s as in any period, can be attributed to an imbalance in percentages of dominant and nondominant women. As a country becomes affluent, the number of births of dominant children falls because dominant women control their fertility. Although unacknowledged, this has been a consistent historical occurrence, especially evident in the upper class. Affluent dominant women frequently have fewer children than dominant women who have not yet attained affluence.

After a country achieves affluence, the number of dominant upper-class members available for marriage shrinks through the withholding of children by dominant, upper-class women. The system begins to deteriorate, and its control over the country diminishes.

Dominant individuals in the upper class, especially men, are the high achievers. When dominant women limit or stop having children during affluent times, it takes only one or two generations before a majority of the class becomes nondominant, that is, fewer members gaining power or fame or achieving and producing wealth. Nondominant individuals can marry each other within the class according to custom, or they can break the class barrier by selecting a dominant marriage partner from a lower class.

When nondominant class members marry, the system can be maintained only temporarily. The children, because of the mother, are nondominant like their parents. If the first nondominant union does not dissipate the family wealth, the second nondominant marriage probably will. Thus, a family could lose everything in only one or two generations. And so it came to pass in England between 1900 and 1950; little more than titles remain of the nobility.

While America claimed freedom from the strictures of class, it nevertheless followed the course of other great societies. Beginning with the ninth generation, 1963 to 1987, substantial inheritances began to move in greater numbers from dominant producers to nondominant scions. Subsequent business failures, misadventures, and wasted inheritances were reported anecdotally; the news media had yet to recognize these events as precursors of an irreversible trend.

America failed to escape the tenth generation's increased ratios of nondominant have-nots versus dominant haves. Nor could the nation extract itself from that generation's historical legacy of transferring the bulk of the last great achievers' wealth and power to squanderers and wastrels. This, too, would come to pass between 1988 and 2012, where there were too few dominant Americans to rebuild family fortunes or create new ones.

The stream of transmitted wealth to spendthrifts swelled to a flood. Between 1988 and 2012, some twenty-five billion ounces of gold would pass from the last achieving generation to charities, foundations, and universities, but chiefly to their descendants — prodigals and high-living spendthrifts. This munificent sum was more than two times the national debt of the United States in July 1995. Having little desire to achieve, but many ideas on how to spend, this new generation frittered away history's largest accumulation of wealth. Some renounced their American citizenship and took their gold to foreign countries. Only a few invested in American industry and the creation of jobs.

No past society came close to equaling the wealth and power amassed by the United States in its first ten-generation epoch. More striking, the plenitude was spread among 20 percent of the population rather than concentrated with a very few. Still the end was the same — achievers to spendthrifts in one generation.

At the same time, entrepreneurial successes glittered, since the small numbers of entrepreneurs limited competition. Other, more established, dominant business leaders capitalized on the decreasing levels of the dominance trait. They paid themselves and their close associates exorbitantly. Further, they instigated corporate takeovers and terminated hundreds of thousands of employees at the taken-over corporations led by less successful leaders. Additionally, the ever-increasing gap between corporate executive officers' pay and workers' salaries hastened the decline in the number of middle-class Americans.

But do not let the excesses of tenth-generation spendthrifts tempt you to tax severely the future transmission of wealth by inheritance. Realize that, had the tenth generation forfeited its inheritance to the government through taxation, little would have changed. The entrenched lawmakers of that very generation would have consumed that wealth also, although in a different manner. Each act to restrict the accumulation and disbursement of wealth weakens the entrepreneurial spirit. Allow high achievers to leave their assets to whom they choose with minimal inheritance taxes. This is far less onerous than dealing with unemployment. Keep death taxes small, especially those of small-business owners and heads of family-owned and operated farms.

Dominant individuals most often acquire wealth to assuage their fear of failure and to satisfy their need to achieve. Since few have the ability to do this alone, employing others to help them accomplish their goals coincides with your need to create gainful employment for all citizens. A dominant person's phobia of being controlled in turn creates the need to control others, a by-product of which is the creation of wealth. You personally foreswore accumulating wealth. But you have power. Permit productive Americans to become rich in gold and worldly goods. Not only will the nation become stronger, but you, Mr. President, will become more powerful.

CHAPTER TWELVE

Restoring Value to American Citizenship

＊

After 1964, as American leaders became complacent, U.S. citizenship lost its value. In my time, foreigners acquired citizenship with ease; it was awarded through amnesty to unlawful aliens already living in the country and sold to wealthy foreigners.

Penniless illegal Hispanic immigrants paid nothing and received amnesty. Prosperous legal immigrants paid by proving a net worth of either 1,300 or 2,600 gold ounces along with a pledge to start up a rural or urban business and employ American workers. Between these extremes, hundreds of thousands of other foreigners found ways, both honest and dishonest, to obtain citizenship.

Without conscience and without historical precedent, Senator Alan K. Simpson's bill granted amnesty to millions of illegal aliens, thus rewarding acknowledged lawbreakers with citizenship. This act announced to the world that an impotent United States could not protect its borders from illegal entry. Whether the purpose of entry was benign or hostile, foreigners could enter and reside in the country at will.

Many new immigrants found freedom from want as recipients of federal and state largess. They merely had to apply to have welfare showered on them. Others found freedom pursuing crime. Lax American justice let newcomers have their way in every form of criminal activity, quite different from the punishment given lawbreakers in their countries of origin. New citizens from these two groups became increasingly parasitic. Not content with what they got — wanting more and getting more became synonymous. The costs of welfare and theft became unbearable. A two-tiered American citizenship emerged: newcomers getting, oldcomers giving.

You began the process of restoring value to American citizenship when you rescinded all laws enacted since 1964. This stopped the depletion of state and federal funds previously wasted on bilingual public schoolteachers to conduct primary classes in Spanish for Hispanic children. Prior to 1964, all immigrants, including those from Spanish-speaking countries, learned American English on their own, and many rose to the highest levels of American success. Forced bilingual education produced a multitude of Hispanic busboys, waiters, and criminals and scarcely any Hispanic scientists. As electives, second languages are excellent opportunities; when mandated as a contrived bridge-language for a group, they confer secondary citizenship.

From this country's early days, Puritan New Englanders, Dutch New York burghers, Pennsylvania Quakers, and aristocratic Southern slaveholders resented each other's cultures, values, and sometimes language. Too many years elapsed, including a civil war, before the United States achieved a single identity and a standard, broad-based culture. Earlier American demands on immigrant groups for assimilation brought benefits for most in the ensuing "melting pot."

American English paved the way for that unification. It began in 1778, eleven years before the Constitution of the United States was ratified, when the Continental Congress decreed that messages to foreign emissaries be issued in the language of the United States. In 1789, 90 percent of the country's Caucasian inhabitants were of English descent. Even then, as new words and meanings were added, American English was changing rapidly from the mother tongue.

Languages have lifetimes: thriving and growing in energetic countries, dying in lethargic ones. During a great nation's growth, words multiply dramatically. In England, few people living in the second generation after Shakespeare could understand the written language of just two generations before Shakespeare. Later, when England declined in prosperity and power, its language stagnated.

Similarly, as America grew, American English mushroomed and its usage worldwide escalated. Theodore Roosevelt was prescient when he stated, "The one absolute certain way of bringing this nation to ruin would be to permit it to become a tangle of squabbling nationalities. We have but one flag. We must also have but one language, and that language is English."

The nation must be unified again. It is a mockery, Mr. President, that you must reinvent this wheel of unity, but reinvent you must. Without action, American citizenship continues to mean little more than a second home for foreigners. Your success and the success of American English are inseparable.

Conduct all business, private and public, in American English. A few newspapers and television and radio stations will test your determination, particularly those with Hispanic audiences. Revoke their licenses, confiscate their assets, and sell them to the highest bidder. Old-fashioned competition provides buyers; let them profit from the stupidity of those who question your resolve.

Deport and revoke the citizenship — which they do not appreciate — of those who agitate for a multicultural and multilingual society instead of assimilation. For those not content to be Americans with one language, one culture, and one identity, but who do not foment unrest, merely encourage them to return to their native homelands.

After 1987, a few American-born citizens renounced their citizenship to avoid federal and state taxes. These wealthy former Americans took advantage of all our nation's good and left with their own goods before the ship sank. Their citizenship meant nothing to them. These turncoat tax avoiders are the easiest to deal with. Ban them from our country and never allow them to return. Prohibit all Americans, even relatives, from transacting business with them. Have the Internal Revenue Service audit every income tax return filed during their lifetime. Apply the penalties set forth in your crime agenda for any criminal actions uncovered in the audit. Bring absentee criminal proceedings against them, as they can never again set foot in America. Sentence those found guilty to confinement in overseas prisons (and expect Africa to be the destination for most). Since they were absent when tried and convicted, they are unlikely to appear on time at the foreign prison gate. Thus, treat them as escaped prisoners — outlaws. Bounty hunters will locate even the most cunning of these fugitives.

Deal differently with other citizenship categories. The prerequisite of losing something is first to have it; one cannot lose what one does not have. Little merit lies in making it harder to acquire American citizenship, while much good lies in taking it away. Demonstrate your determination to restore the value of American citizenship through your actions.

Revoke the citizenship of all immigrants who became American citizens after 1964 and who, as citizens, received a felony conviction. Return those not in prison to their native countries with seventy-two hours' deportation notice. They can settle their American affairs from their home country. Family members residing in the United States can join the felons in the old country or decide not to follow those felonious ways and remain as law-abiding American citizens. Regardless of country of origin, treat all revoked citizenships equally, without appeal.

Make one exception, however, for the country of Nigeria. Immigrants and visitors from no other country equal the percentage of upper-class Nigerian crooks in the United States. They are world-class masters of white-collar theft and financial scams. Upper-class Nigerian culture lauds dishonesty more than does any other nation. Rarely is anyone so displeased at having his own things stolen to the extent that upper-class Nigerians are displeased at not having stolen someone else's goods. In my time, it was stated that over 75 million ounces of gold were looted from Nigeria by government officials, most sent to Switzerland. Six thousand Nigerians were reported to be worth over 2.5 million gold ounces each. Another six thousand were said to have a net worth far exceeding 2,500 gold ounces each, and fifty-five thousand were reported to have a net worth of at least 2,500 gold ounces each. At the same time, 22 million poor Nigerians each earned slightly more than one ounce of gold per year.

Every former Nigerian who became an American citizen after 1964, his descendants, and his relatives should have their American citizenships revoked and be deported to Nigeria within forty-eight hours. Revoke old visas and deny new visas; have no involvement with Nigeria. With one stroke you stop Nigerians from ever pirating Americans again. Let other countries cope with Nigeria's culture.

Americans and the world will soon see that what was given freely can be withdrawn just as easily. You have the power to rescind the citizenship of individuals or the entire American population emanating from specific countries. Having restored value to U.S. citizenship, you will benefit immediately from the new-found pride in being an American. World leaders will reassess your resolve. You also serve notice globally that you, America's Man on Horseback, can and will act decisively and move quickly without the restraint of politics.

CHAPTER THIRTEEN

Appeasement

❧

When Carthage paid the last of her fifty annual indemnities
of 200 talents to Rome, she felt herself released from the
treaty signed after Zama. In 151 she declared war against
Numidia, and a year later Rome declared war against her.

The latter declaration, and the news that the Roman fleet
had already sailed for Africa, reached Carthage at the same
time. The ancient city, however rich in population and
trade, was quite unprepared for a major war. She had a
small army, a smaller navy, no mercenaries, no allies. Rome
controlled the sea. Utica therefore declared for Rome, and
Masinissa blocked all egress from Carthage to the
hinterland. An embassy hastened to Rome with authority to
meet all demands. The Senate promised that if Carthage
would turn over to the Roman consuls in Sicily 300 children
of the noblest families as hostages, and would obey whatever
orders the consuls would give, the freedom and territorial
integrity of Carthage would be preserved. Secretly the Senate
bade the consuls carry out the instructions that they had
already received. The Carthaginians gave up their children
with forebodings and laments; the relatives crowded the
shores in a despondent farewell; at the last moment the
mothers tried by force to prevent the ships from sailing; and
some swam out to sea to catch a last glimpse of their
children. The consuls sent the hostages to Rome, crossed to
Utica with army and fleet, summoned the Carthaginian
ambassadors, and required of Carthage the surrender of her
remaining ships, a great quantity of grain, and all her
engines and weapons of war. When these conditions had
been fulfilled, the consuls further demanded that the
population of Carthage should retire to ten miles from the
city, which was then to be burned to the ground. The
ambassadors argued in vain that the destruction of a city
which had surrendered hostages and its arms without

*striking a blow was a treacherous atrocity unknown to
history. They offered their own lives as a vicarious
atonement; they flung themselves upon the ground and beat
the earth with their heads. The consuls replied that the
terms were those of the Senate and could not be changed.*

*When the people of Carthage heard what was demanded
of them they lost their sanity. Parents mad with grief tore
limb from limb the leaders who had advised surrendering
the child hostages; others killed those who had counseled the
surrender of arms; some dragged the returning ambassadors
through the streets and stoned them; some killed whatever
Italians could be found in the city; some stood in the empty
arsenals and wept. The Carthaginian Senate declared war
against Rome and called all adults — men and women,
slave or free — to form a new army, and to forge anew the
weapons of defense. Fury gave them resolution. Public
buildings were demolished to provide metal and timber; the
statues of cherished gods were melted down to make swords,
and the hair of the women was shorn to make ropes. In two
months the beleaguered city produced 8000 shields, 18,000
swords, 30,000 spears, 60,000 catapult missiles, and built in
its inner harbor a fleet of 120 ships.*

*Three years the city stood siege by land and sea. . . . At
last the population, reduced from 500,000 to 55,000,
surrendered. Hasdrubal, their general, pleaded for his life,
which Scipio granted, but his wife, denouncing his
cowardice, plunged with her sons into the flames. The
survivors were sold as slaves, and the city was turned over to
the legions for pillage.*

WILL DURANT,
CAESAR AND CHRIST
THE STORY OF CIVILIZATION, PART III

Carthage could have observed the treaty, minded its own business, and left Numidia alone. Having instead chosen to initiate a war and indirectly challenge Rome, Carthage's decision then to appease Rome turned a poor choice into a historical disaster. Appeasement is the hallmark of weak and timid leaders. Its bloody footprints track through history, staining first this and then that nation. While appeasement begins quietly, it ends calamitously; accommodation satisfies only the appeaser as concessions whet the appetite of the instigator. Prime Minister Neville Chamberlain had Great Britain stand aside to mollify Adolf Hitler. Germany's "man on horseback" accepted from Chamberlain the lands he wanted in Czechoslovakia; later he demanded all of Poland. Standing firm and not appeasing Hitler would have accelerated Britain's war preparations and saved countless lives. Chamberlain was voted out, Winston Churchill voted in. Appeasement ceased, war began, and Germany lost everything.

History finds no heroes among appeasers, only cowards. Acts of appeasement sometimes take a century to reverse, but sooner or later the price for placation is paid. Appeasement always brings misfortune to the people, who suffer more as time passes, for the price paid to escape boxes and traps is always cheapest at inception and becomes more dear with each passing day. The mediating leaders themselves rarely suffer; they usually die peacefully in bed. Because of the past cowardly actions of conciliatory leaders, future generations suffer misery. In the case of the Carthaginians, retribution against such leaders came in their lifetimes — too late, but not too little.

For eight generations, American citizens living at home and abroad were protected. They traveled unmolested through developed foreign nations and moved with relative safety in primitive countries. Even during the hazardous settlement of the western United States, only a few hundred pioneer settlers lost their lives in Indian raids. Within the U.S. borders, law enforcement and swift justice ensured dependable security. Foreign safe shelter occurred not because of the peacefulness of alien countries but due to the almost sacrosanct quality of being an American. Between 1812 and 1964, American civilians traveling abroad were enveloped in the aura of the power of the United States.

After 1964, however, the safety of Americans deteriorated at home and abroad. The resolve and steadfastness of the nation's leaders dwindled, slipping steadily until your advent. No American president of those years had the strength of character to maintain the determination of earlier heads of state. Concession, conciliation, placation, and propitiation became the American way to disguise the country's ripening rot. The nation's softening of resolve in foreign affairs was the harbinger of appeasement.

Indeed, foreign aid, a plague that the United States avoided for 169 years, represents a special form of appeasement. There is no surer way to lose respect, enrich greedy foreign rulers, and create resentment than through foreign aid. Aid to developing countries never produced a single country that moved from the developing to the developed stage. Developing countries remain in this state and collect foreign aid as long as nations continue to confer such funds. Appeasement within the United States also was rampant during my time. Domestic white flags of government dole and affirmative action fueled ethnic dissatisfaction and kindled race riots.

Only countries with more gold than good sense practice such benevolent bestowing. In my time, the United States borrowed money to fund foreign aid. Recognizing public resentment of such funding, politicians became adroit at hiding their foreign favors. Burying such bequests under "promoting peace" and "defense" was a popular political ploy. With no more gold and without the ability to borrow, undoubtedly you, Mr. President, will end foreign aid and discharge those bureaucrats paid to give it away.

Domestic accommodation and foreign aid along with foreign compromise were interpreted, inside and outside the United States, as weaknesses inviting more abuses. The nation soothed foreign buyers of American debt by accepting unfair trade practices from those countries. Presidents gave elaborate apologies to foreign leaders for trivial occurrences caused by American citizens.

Appeasement never delivers the hoped-for promise; it only kindles a desire for what previously was thought to be unattainable.

CHAPTER FOURTEEN

End Foreign Terrorism —
Prepare the Military for Profit

𝕏

A strong indication of the deterioration of our nation's inner strength is its overuse of amnesty. You will be inundated with clamors for coming together, healing, forgiving, pardoning, excusing, making America whole, and dozens of other ideas for class amnesty. (Presidential pardons pose no problems if conferred to an individual instead of a class. An individual will praise your forbearance; a group will not.) Granting amnesty to citizens who commit offenses against the U.S. government is an act of cowardice, for it serves only to embolden current lawbreakers and set precedents for future law-mockers. Not an act of compassion, amnesty merely lays bare weakness and gives heart to the enemies of our nation, thus your enemies. Further, amnesty robs you of future legitimate action; for without it, each group will go to greater lengths not to offend you. (Remember, however, that in some instances laws may have been broken on your behalf. So while amnesty is to be avoided, you may decide without announcement to postpone or not to pursue this or that class of lawbreakers.)

Particularly damaging, in the nation's past, were across-the-board pardons for those who refused to fight for their country and amnesty for those who fled the United States to avoid military duty. Each time amnesty was granted, it was under the guise of "a time to come together, a time for healing." Nothing was healed, however, since anonymity was given to cowards, which hindered any coming together or healing between those who served their country and those who did not, as too few Americans knew the names of the draft dodgers who ran away. Anonymity denied Americans the choice of either forgiving or shunning. These actions encourage the weakhearted to shirk their duties.

The nation's abundance and wealth provided comforts and conveniences that weakened the physical stamina and moral fiber of American citizens. Americans became too soft and comfortable; they no longer realized what war was. (The military was not exempt. In 1992, for the first time in U.S. naval history, a sailor gave birth to a baby aboard ship.) Far too many took pride and comfort in decisive victories in the invasion of Grenada, the Persian Gulf War, and the invasions of Panama and Somalia. Three generations before, Americans considered similar minor military actions "gunboat diplomacy," not war.

NATIONS, like trees, die from the top down. Seeing only the trunk, the country's citizens rarely notice the withering leaves seen by those far away. Beetles and birds ravage dying trees; human predators feast on dying societies. And so the end of ten-generation cycles invariably brings voracious intervening foreigners who meddle and plot against decadent cultures in their weakened and waning final two generations. Without exception, intervention occurs.

Fourteen countries intrigued over the remains of Romanov Russia. Near the end of the C'hing (Manchu) Dynasty, China became the object of a feeding frenzy by foreign countries. A vigorous America schemed near the end of both floundering societies and was the prime meddler in Japan's last ten-generation cycle, which ended in 1868.

A more resolute, pre-1950 England had no tolerance for foreign intervention or terrorism. But England lost its way, and the country lay open for intruders from all nations to have their way. England's most recent ten-generation cycle began in 1700. This magnificent country became Great Britain, and men of boundless will brought 25 percent of the world under her domain. Nearly one-third of all current sovereign countries worldwide were once colonies or protectorates of Great Britain. In my time they still met regularly as a group, a constant reminder of the extent to which Great Britain was no longer great. The law of ten generations had its way, ending the cycle in 1950.

Already swollen with unwanted immigrants, the English suffered at the hands of unwanted Irish terrorists. Government leaders possessed the power to stop terrorism but lacked the will. Whispers of retaliation against Ireland melted away, while negotiations with terrorist leaders brought only sporadic interludes of peace. Nations throughout the world quietly supported Ireland's thugs and their cause. American presidents John Kennedy and William Clinton dabbled in Ireland's affairs. President Clinton went so far as to invite Ireland's leading terrorist to the United States, treating him as visiting royalty, while an impotent Britain stood silent. U.S. citizens contributed the most to Irish terrorists, funneling thousands of gold ounces through the Northern Ireland Aid Committee (NORAID) to Ireland's murderers and giving even more directly.

During America's twilight phase, foreign intervention was inevitable, although the methods of meddling, other than bribing American politicians, were unpredictable. While America's armament stayed the hand of alien armies, terrorism became the tool of choice for interloping foreign governments. Foreign terrorists attacked the very roots of the United States. In my time, the successes in faraway countries of automobiles laden with crude explosives were copied in the United States by terrorists. More than a few Americans dreaded the time when cheap, Chinese-made land mines would be sowed indiscriminately and reap a harvest of maimed and dead. Some feared that more sophisticated weapons were in the offing: foreign terrorists redirecting American-designed hand-held missiles at American airplanes in flight, here and abroad, and nuclear bombs miniaturized and used in America.

The federal government's retaliation against countries funding terrorism was nil. Terrorists' home countries were bombarded with nothing more than signals, verbal sanctions, unenforced boycotts, and empty threats. Politicians dared not use the term *kidnap victim* for fear of inciting Americans and offending foreign governments. They preferred the euphemism — *hostage*. This seemed to imply some legitimacy for the acts of terrorists instead of immediately branding these acts as kidnappings by criminals. In my time, the U.S. government under President Ronald Reagan rewarded kidnappers of Americans by offering Iran arms in exchange for the victims. At home in America, flags were flown at half-mast, national moments of silence were honored, and citizens were encouraged to display yellow ribbons in support of victims. One far-fetched presidential proposal suggested that citizens light candles and place them in the windows of their homes to show support for the "hostages." After a lighted candle caused a home to burn down, that idea lost ground.

Terrorist bombings heightened divisiveness, the ultimate purpose of foreign aggression. State governors already imitated barons of old, flexing their muscles as the king, the federal government, weakened. Without realizing their status as temporarily living branches of the dying tree, state leaders made much of the federal government's inability to protect its citizens. State governments joined federal security forces to devise elaborate and complicated defenses against foreign terrorism. A few plans were implemented; still fewer succeeded. No state government managed to halt domestic crime, much less foreign terrorism; they knew only how to build prisons. States lacked the wisdom, power, and authority to retaliate against foreign countries; the federal government lacked the will.

You have accomplished much in a short time; however, this falls short in protecting America against foreign intervention. Alien eyes filled with envy incessantly search for weaknesses to turn to their advantage. They see American impotence without the prospect of restored virility. America was crippled and despairing at your arrival. You crushed domestic terrorism, violence, and crime; now you must protect Americans from foreign terrorism abroad and at home.

Since you are from the military, you know that military superiority requires matchless technological weaponry and second-to-none fighting men. Therefore, I need offer little counsel. However, I do propose a few thoughts for your consideration as commander in chief.

The peacekeeping efforts of armed forces lead nowhere, cost

money, and insulate the country's servicemen from the reality of war. American soldiers need experience fighting, not pouring oil on troubled waters. Armed intervention in a foreign country provides a laboratory in which to test new weapons and a way to maintain a cutting edge on warrior skills.

Be selective. Evaluate the potential good and bad of a conflict, and consider whether America as a whole, or any of its individual citizens, is threatened. If so, move in. If a country requests intervention by the United States but such interference does not fit the test, stay out. (This test will rarely suit the agendas of allies, but allies are forever changing.) Should you choose not to intervene, sell arms to both sides, equally, and befriend both as they pursue war. Our nation's weaponry factories can evaluate product effectiveness at the same time that America prospers through armament sales.

Intervene immediately to protect Americans and their assets or to prevent the disruption of strategic supplies, such as oil. Move quickly with your arsenal of men and weapons. Though you must win at whatever the cost in lives, avoid either an overkill or an underkill; establish in advance an acceptable ratio of American men-at-arms who may expire in combat.

If few or no American lives are lost while the enemy counts 100,000 dead, you are waging butchery or retaliation, not war. Most assuredly such an occasion presents a fine opportunity to test state-of-the-art weaponry, but it does nothing to gauge the mettle of fighting men. The will of your warriors and their commanders constitutes the true strength of your armed services. They must be tested over and over again and their killing expertise honed and stropped while their resolve to win or die hardens. At the other extreme, a loss of one American to every one enemy — or even close to that ratio — is unacceptable. Consider a ratio of one to one hundred. Withhold or increase the use of the technological weapons at your disposal to keep the ratio constant. This battle-tests men under fire, where bravery alone makes the difference. A further benefit: when individual battles unfavorably skew the numbers of Americans lost, courageous and valiant soldiers come to light.

When foreign terrorists threaten American lives, an immediate military response is required. Foreign terrorist groups have never been secret organizations nor kept their source of funding concealed. Strike the country providing the money. The quicker the better.

This forceful measure carries risks. The citizens of countries whose governments support or permit terrorist kidnappings set an exceptionally low value on human life. Maximum punishment there, whether military or civilian, is expected and accepted. The danger in striking back lies in a too-small retaliation. Blow-for-blow retaliation ignites hatred and stiffens resolve, thereby defeating the purpose of reprisals. Do not negotiate for kidnap victims; instead, establish an advance ratio of kidnapping to retaliation for foreigners who hold Americans. When exacting retribution, add civilians with the military count, since, worldwide, life becomes less valuable each year. Expunging five hundred citizens of that terrorist nation per kidnapped American could suffice for the first redress. Charge one thousand lives each for that country's second kidnapping and five thousand for the third. Be prepared to declare war on any country that shrugs off three American kidnapping re-payments. But to show your preference for avoiding war, escalate retribution before invasion. Collect fifty thousand souls as payment for the fourth kidnapping venture and wait.

Invade a country only after a fifth kidnapping. But after conquering the country, you need not establish control. Simply ensure that Americans are respected and will not be kidnapped again. After making sure that all terrorists gave up their ghosts, let the strongest opposing faction eliminate the nation's former leaders as they choose and allow the new leaders to take full credit for their actions. Do not concern yourself with rebuilding the country or its new political structure or the new leadership; the new rulers will be no better than the old. Remove American troops at the earliest possible date. Further, assess the new government a sum equal to twice America's costs of the conflict. You need no monumental ceremony and signing of reparations, only the payments when due. Dare they not pay? And with the government busying itself levying taxes and searching for other sources of revenue to pay reparations, little time remains for the new regime to meet or plot with terrorists to kidnap citizens of the United States.

Deny this degree of self-control to nations that spawn terrorists who murder Americans on American soil. Change the ratios and

the tolerance period. De-cease one thousand of that nation's population per American lost during the first terrorist act and 2,500 per
American for the second incident. Although extremely unlikely,
an especially rabid ruler might permit three terrorist bombings on
American soil. Should a third bombing take place — whether one,
one hundred, or one thousand American lives are taken — wreak
havoc on that nation. Have no tolerance. The United States has
been invaded. Steel your heart, Mr. President, and eradicate at
least five thousand residents of that country for each American life
lost during the third terrorist assault on U.S. soil.

If terrorists take many lives in the third terrorist assault on U.S.
soil, there is little need to invade, as American armed forces would
only be put in harm's way. Use sufficient nuclear deployment in si-
multaneous strikes to bring about satisfactory retaliation ratios.
Facing such resolve and iron will, even the most anti-American
country with nuclear weaponry will stand down rather than attack
the United States of America.

Early warnings to world leaders by setting forth retaliation ratios
should give pause to many American-hating heads of state. Still, a
few may test your mettle. But as the price exacted for kidnapping
and terrorism escalates, the tolerance of foreign leaders for their
extremist residents should diminish. Either that or the inhabitants
themselves will rise up and destroy their leaders.

Large-scale retaliation, whether to end foreign kidnapping of
Americans or terrorist activities in the United States, showcases
the nation's might and your mettle. Ending kidnappings and foreign terrorist murders will earn you respect from abroad and pride
at home. Most importantly, each use of force sharpens the readi-
ness of your troops and smooths your political path for future conquest for profit, not protection. In good time, you will usher in the
Empire's new Age of Conquest.

CHAPTER FIFTEEN

The False Concept of Race

❧

The ploy of pitting American "races" against each other began as a divisive game played for political profit. In time, however, race riots and race-related gang wars made the game politically unrewarding. As president, you inherited a race-based plague of epidemic proportions. Perhaps I can give you a more realistic understanding of human variations on which to base your racial decisions, as the generally accepted world concept of race and attendant racial assumptions are false, including attempts to ally race with intelligence and achievement.

Evolution acknowledges that visible physiological human differences occur and are transmitted through genes from generation to generation. This knowledge leads many scholars and scientists to conclude that genes are also the major determinant in the distribution of intelligence and achievement among the earth's population.

Another element of confusion lies in the word "race." The concept of "race" or "racial origin" is a contemporary one. Racial determination, from its inception and as it exists today, occupies a minuscule time frame in the evolutionary process relative to the millennia humans have occupied the earth.

Possibly the concept of "race" began with Aristotle, was then passed to Bernier in 1684, to Linnaeus in 1735, thence to Buffon in 1749. However, both Linnaeus and Buffon knew that all humans belonged to a single species. Buffon used the term "race" for convenience only.

In the essay "The Concept of Race in the Human Species in the Light of Genetics" from *The Concept of Race* (1964), Ashley Montagu states: "To sum up, the indictment against the anthropological conception of race is (1) that it is artificial; (2) that it does not agree with the facts; (3) that it leads to confusion and the perpetuation of error, and finally, that for all these reasons it is meaningless, or rather more accurately such meaning as it possesses is false. Being so weighed down with false meaning it were better that the term were dropped altogether than that any attempt should be made to give it a new meaning." Montagu notes that past scholars critical of the concept of "race" included Franz Boas, Blumenbach, Joseph Deniker, William Flower, Alfred Haddon, Herder, Lancelot Hogben, Julian Huxley, and T. H. Huxley.

Geography is the primary factor for identifying "racial origin" and "races," including: African Negroids, American Indians, Asian Mongoloids, Australoids, European Caucasoids, Melanesians, Micronesians, and Polynesians. But there is no evidence, for example, that American Indians existed as a "race" thirty thousand years ago. And no biological basis exists for determining "race."

And while biological evolution is assumed to be occurring, the rate of change is imperceptible. Cultural rather than biological evolution has been the primary cause of change in human societies for at least the past thirty thousand years and especially the past ten thousand years. The difference in thoughts and attitudes among diverse groups of people, psychological mankind, result from cultural rather than biological transmission. *There is no evidence of the influence of biological evolution on human affairs during these periods.*

Further, the physiological trait of color is easily traced. Ancient humans and their descendants who remained in the direct sunlight of equatorial Africa retained their dark skin. The descendants of those who moved further north adapted to the lesser amounts of sunlight by gradually lightened skin color, which corresponded in degree according to the distance moved from the tropics. Latitude determined skin color. Other recognizable evolutionary changes include exterior facial features and hair.

We readily accept that nature adjusts animal color in accordance with environmental need. For example, the arctic rabbit is white in winter and brown in summer; this is a proven annual occurrence that people willingly acknowledge. Yet many find it strange to think that ancient black men became brown, then tan, then white after they settled in different latitudes. To some it is simply unbelievable; to many it is emotionally unacceptable. As Arthur Schopenhauer states in *Supplements to the World as Will and Idea*, "the white color of the skin is not natural to man, . . . by nature he has a black or brown skin, . . . consequently a white man has never originally sprung from the womb of nature, . . . there is no such thing as a white race, . . . every white man is a faded or bleached one."

Skeletal construction has been the same in all humans for at least thirty thousand years. Today human bone configurations, including the skull, reflect little or no changes among populations. They are the same for Africans and for those living in northern areas such as Sweden.

T H E phrase "nature versus nurture" is euphonious but also latitudinal and ambiguous. "Heredity versus environment" places a simple concept (heredity) against an all-encompassing one (environment). "The word 'environment,' which is deliberately imprecise," writes Albert Jacquard, "covers such things as the nourishment absorbed . . . the radiation he was exposed to, the shocks he endured, the affection with which he was surrounded, the teaching, of all kinds, which he was given: in short, all the physical and moral influences which shaped the individual in the course of its development from the embryo."

Perhaps the phrase *heredity versus child-rearing practices* is more descriptive when contemplating the origins of intelligence and achievement. Such a comparison counters the premise of sociobiologists that "genes hold the culture on a leash." Despite all their Mendelian formulas, hereditarians cannot gauge adult success at childhood. Child-rearing practices offer an uncomplicated guide for estimating the adult achievement level of a child: look to the successes or failures of the mother's brothers.

Technology presents an analogy. Computer hardware is dormant and unproductive by itself, as is computer software. Only when software is introduced to hardware will the computer function and produce. Could the human body and brain be compared to hardware and child-rearing practices and education to computer software?

CHAPTER SIXTEEN

Race, Culture, and Child-Rearing Practices

❧

From Stone Age tools to agriculture to the founding of the world's first city, from the building of the great pyramids to smelting copper, from bronze to iron — human achievement tracked north and northeast from mankind's east African beginnings. Thus, as great empires rose and fell — Mesopotamia, Egypt, China, Greece, Etruria, and Rome, just as in more recent centuries it was evident in Spain and England, and so for Europe, the United States, and Japan — success was predisposed to those groups in each era with decreasing amounts of pigmentation in their skin. For thousands of years, these successes of human achievement and acumen were attributed to "race."

Man's analysis over time of the cause of lightning and thunder differs little. The work of pagan gods was answer enough for ancient man. While science provides more sophisticated answers for the phenomenon, it does not change the occurrence — it is still lightning and thunder. And there are still differences in levels of achievement among ethnic groups and races, with only trifling changes in mindset and wrong conclusions.

Regardless of the reasons, along each step of civilization's journey north, enclaves of lighter-skinned people were dramatically more successful than their darker-skinned counterparts. Superior and innovative artifacts from different geographic locations in the

111

same time periods make this statement irrefutable. Nothing changed regardless of ancient or modern explanations.

Among the darkest of the dark-skinned are Negroes. Explanations for their lesser achievements over time are no more logical today than they were hundreds of years ago. When comparing achievement and "race," it would be less harmful to "know" nothing than to "know" something that is false. Of course, so-called reasons abound — Negroes are the descendants of Canaan, the fourth son of Ham, cursed by Noah, father of Ham; their brain matter weighs less or is of a different quality than that of those with lighter skin color; they occupy a later place in evolutionary development; and so forth. Anthropologists contribute greatly to the last supposition. Some pretend that Negroes occupy a later place in evolutionary development, instead of making public that all people were dark in color at the beginning of mankind on earth. They sketch Neanderthal man as brutish in appearance and dark in color, while portraying Cro-Magnon man as modern in mien and light in color. South Africa's Cro-Magnon man is never depicted, since he would have had dark-colored skin. Few anthropologists acknowledge that light-colored skin is merely an environmental adaptation that occurred when the more dominant among dark-colored humans migrated northward less than one million years ago. No anthropologist ever published estimates of the number of generations of black-in-color ancestors in the family trees of all light-in-color people living today.

(Partial enlightenment comes many times from unlikely sources. In 1996, Pope John Paul II proclaimed that the Church accepted the theory of evolution with qualifications. However, the pronouncement did not address whether Adam and Eve were black in color.)

Even recent historical events give the lie to "race" and show also how transparent the use of religious, tribal, or ethnic terms is when substituted for dominance levels. In Ireland, when the nondominant Irish majority war with the more dominant English-Irish minority, differences are charged to religion, since both groups are Caucasian. When religious lines blur, "ethnic differences" become the catch-all term to encompass the carnage among Caucasians. When the nondominant Rwanda Hutu majority kill hundreds of thousands of the dominant Tutsi minority, who in turn kill a still larger number of Hutus, the blame is placed on tribal clashes, as all adversaries are Negroes.

"Racism" is the term used worldwide to denote strife between light- and dark-colored people. Bloodbaths among different South African tribes are called tribal conflicts, while an equal slaughter between South African Caucasians and Negroes is ascribed to racism.

> Caucasian versus Caucasian: religion, ethnicity, genocide, gangs
> Negro versus Negro: tribes, gangs
> Caucasian versus Negro: racism
> Negro versus Caucasian: antiracism

Individuals and groups with high needs for achievement, the dominant, control those who have less need to achieve, the nondominant. This holds true without regard to tribes, skin color, religion, or ethnicity. Nature does not deviate: life must breed, and Nature is more interested in the species than the individual. She likes large litters. In humans, the nondominant are prolific breeders while the more dominant are frugal with their issue. Nature makes no distinction among illiterate/literate, disobedient/obedient, lawbreakers/law-abiders, shiftless/industrious, or shades of color. Without fail, Nature rewards prolific human breeders by ensuring that their progeny will be the ultimate inheritors of this world.

Consequently, countries are repeatedly in a stage of flux between the nondominant have-nots and the dominant haves. Even countries with homogeneous color, culture, and religion, which from time to time appear safe within their borders, are not spared this ebb and flow from within and without. Signposts of sovereignty receive little heed when nondominant breeders search for food and shelter or when dominant groups seek conquest.

Differences in achievement among all people of all skin colors — black, white, and shades in between — have nothing to do with "race" and everything to do with child-rearing practices. Politicians knew this but averred that they did not. They played games among themselves. Liberals since 1964 responded to nondominant (low-achieving) child-rearing practices with programs that ignored the "why" of the problems and addressed only the symptoms. Conservatives, in turn, blamed the liberal social programs as the "why" of the problems. Important liberal and conservative politicians knew better, as each knew how he personally was reared.

Politicians and judges worked hard for years to prevent adoptions by qualified Caucasian parents of Negro and American Indian children. In their view, it was far better to have the children reared in cultural darkness and ignorance than to watch Caucasian parents, whether the mother was dominant or nondominant, rear a higher percentage of them for adult success. The magnitude of the differing degrees of child-rearing practices could give the game away.

Negro leaders strove to preserve and bequeath their positions of power to family members, not increase competition. At the same time, Caucasian Americans' bigoted fears of a dominant Negro ruling class thwarted any possibility of Caucasian private funding for child-rearing schools designed to produce a Negro elite. Many Caucasians resisted so strongly the idea of intelligent, dominant, successful Negroes that they genuinely preferred to fear ignorant and violent Negro criminals than admit Negroes as equals or, much worse, superiors.

American leaders, including Negro leaders, knew all along that child-rearing practices separated the dominant haves from the nondominant have-nots. They realized that they themselves were among the persons of large account who had mothers who made many demands for early achievement. They saw that those of little account had mothers who made few demands of them for accomplishments while young. It did not escape them that mothers of no-account people made no demands for childhood performance.

The importance of child-rearing practices can be seen in the example of Jews, who have an unbroken four-thousand-year history of success. No other group, race, or civilization comes close. Halacha holds that children of a Jewish mother are Jewish regardless of the father's religious faith; lineage is traced through the mother. Almost without exception, every Jew attaining by his own efforts money, power, or fame was reared by a dominant mother or maternal grandmother who enforced dominant child-rearing practices. Many successful Jews, particularly men, take personal credit for their achievements, not according recognition to the role of the child-rearing methods that conditioned them to be achievers.

Dominant women rear dominant daughters as well as dominant sons. Although marriages between dominant and nondominant individuals occur in all cultures, the effects are most noticeable in an extremely intelligent and dominant group such as American Jews. So long as successful Jewish men marry within their religion, they are likely to marry dominant women. The attitudes that lead to success will thus be instilled in the next generation. However, during the past two generations, interfaith marriages between American Jewish men and gentile women increased dramatically. Dominant, aggressive, successful, and therefore prosperous, Jewish men now marry nondominant gentile women, deliberately breaking the marriage laws of Halacha. As a result, their offspring, reared by nondominant mothers with different child-rearing methods, will not achieve the same level of success as did the father. Do they realize this outcome? If so, this is hubris in its keenest form.

The possibility that slavery existed in human prehistory cannot be denied. "Slavery was a universal institution throughout ancient times. It was not even questioned in the Old Testament or in the New Testament," so wrote Isaac Asimov. Jews were slaves. Negroes were taken from Africa against their will and, like the Jews, were spread around the world against their will. Each group took its culture, and thus child-rearing practices, with it. Racial differences do not separate them; it is the profound cultural differences, brought about by child-rearing practices alone, that make them so different.

A culture of ignorance is perpetuated through child-rearing practices regardless of nationality, skin color, or geographic location.

When Negroes arrived unwillingly in America, they brought with them child-rearing practices developed over thousands of years. Child-rearing methods practiced by most of Africa's present Negro population are similar to those currently practiced by many American Negroes. Over the years, the ratio of dominant versus nondominant Negroes has changed little in America from that in

Africa. Regardless of skin color or ethnicity, only the truly ignorant are unaware of their ignorance.

Saying *no* and exacting obedience to *no* are entirely different actions. The preponderance of nondominant mothers cannot bring themselves to actually enforce the limits of *no* with their offspring. These children of nondominant mothers learn that although they are told *no*, they are not required to obey; they may continue their actions without penalty. Many times when such children are punished, sometimes severely, the reasons are capricious, because of the mother's anger or whim, and are unrelated to establishing clear and consistent rules of conduct.

Consequently, demands for preschool excellence in tying shoelaces, distinguishing colors, telling time, reading, writing, proper grammar, good diction, and good manners do not receive the necessary follow-through and so are missing from generation to generation. (Regardless of ethnicity, American adults who achieve these preschool accomplishments may pay vast sums in taxes, but they do not collect welfare.)

Negro adults with outstanding accomplishments are no different from high achievers of other ethnicities: they too stem from more dominant mothers. Dominant Negro mothers produce immensely successful offspring, but they remain a minuscule percentage of Negro female parents. A count of high-level corporate executives, commercial pilots, surgeons, admirals and generals, professors teaching in the hundred highest-rated universities, certified public accountants, and business owners finds less than 2 percent of American Negroes as having dominant mothers who instilled in them needs for high achievement.

Public schoolteachers of my day were so intimidated that they accepted disobedient behavior by Negro youths as a right of the "black culture." Further, juvenile crime became so pervasive that police and judges excepted from prosecution many criminal activities committed by Negro preteens and teens. Lawmakers were far too tolerant of crimes committed by Negro youth. But at some time, someone, to some degree, had to say no and enforce it.

This happened eventually when Negroes committed heinous crimes. Sullen and surprised when arrested, numerous Negro (and Caucasian) criminals blamed the victim for resisting armed robbery, rape, or even murder. Slain innocent bystanders were dismissed with "they should not have been there, they were unlucky." Attorneys representing Negro criminals pleaded for not-guilty verdicts, deferred adjudication, probation, community service, or short sentences because the criminal "was the product of a bad environment and had no opportunity to better himself."

No particular group of individuals has ever been free from discrimination or slavery throughout written history. Further, no descendants of former slaves, regardless of ethnicity, ever reaped financial rewards based solely on having had slave ancestors, and few reparations have ever been paid because of past discrimination. That is, until 1964 in the United States.

Lawmakers from 1964 forward passed law after law to "rectify past discrimination" against American Negroes. In return, Negroes concentrated their votes to reward and retain those politicians. During the race to rectify past discrimination, politicians left no stone unturned in their efforts to create equality. Thus, rectifying past discrimination begot reverse discrimination, which became a way of life. Federal, state, and private-sector affirmative action programs, university enrollment quotas, federal contracts-with-the-government quotas, and doing-business-with-the-state quotas gave Negroes an unfair advantage over other Americans.

"Race norming" is a particularly insidious form of equalization used on employment tests. In *Paved with Good Intentions* Jared Taylor noted that "The technique is simply to give blacks or Hispanics higher marks than whites for the same number of correct answers." A multitude of Caucasian job seekers competing with Negroes and Hispanics never know why they fail to win federal, state, and even some private-sector jobs. But their eyes and minds confirm that many Negroes and Hispanics, though less qualified, secure the same jobs. This is most evident among Caucasians failing to obtain jobs with the United States Postal Service.

Bestowing unearned largess on the undeserving, whether to a relative or a member of a specific group, may satisfy the bestower, but it fosters resentment in the recipient. The undeserving person welcomes but sees little good in what is received, since the desire for more occupies his mind. In these instances, the good to the beneficiary is wasted, as it only highlights the possibility of more.

Since it is undeserved, so goes the logic, it becomes wrong for the giver to set a limit.

Generations-ago wrongs, real and imagined, were overcompensated by new laws with the full enforcement of the United States government. All segments of American industry along with the federal and state bureaucracies were brought to heel. Correcting social imbalances gave underqualified Negroes little job or educational satisfaction but produced much anger. Since 1964, American Negroes in their anger perceived racism at every turn. Little escaped their attention. The preponderance of Negro and Caucasian marriages occur between Negro men and Caucasian women; few marriages take place between Caucasian men and Negro women. According to Jared Taylor, "In 1988, for example, there were 9,406 reported cases of whites being raped by blacks, whereas there were *fewer than* 10 reported cases of blacks being raped by whites." Although these numbers came from estimates derived from a complex sample survey, Caucasian men do practice racism in their marriages and in their rapes while Negro men do not.

In "righting" these perceived "wrongs," lawmakers shackled the United States. The federal government intimidated and coerced the non-Negro population from 1964 to my time. At the same time, Negroes set records for belligerence and crime. During this period, America's decadent society went to such lengths to embrace free speech that five four-letter words that in earlier times were taboo dropped to two and then none. However, new taboo words surfaced: "shiftless" disappeared from use, and particularly taboo was "nigger" when spoken by anyone except a Negro.

A M E R I C A' S language is rich, colorful, and regional. Southerners find "youse" as in "youse guys" amusing, and in the South "bogey man" becomes "booger man." Northerners cannot decode the South's use of "yall" as in "yall come," thinking it means "you all." "Yall" is simply a contraction of "all of you," little different than "goodbye," which contracts "God be with you" and the Spanish *adios,* which contracts *Vaya con Dios.*

We share a propensity to add and subtract consonants to and from spoken words. Many people in New York and New Jersey use the "hard r" in their speech. Idea becomes "idear." In the South, wash becomes "warsh," while rinse sounds like "rinch." Southern Negroes frequently add or subtract the letter "r" when speaking. In food, pork becomes "pok." With automobile names, Ford sounds like "Foad," Buick becomes "Burick," and Dodge is pronounced "Dorge."

Contractions, expansions, and corruptions of the spoken word go back as far as language itself. In 1619 the first twenty dark-skinned Africans were traded and sold in Virginia; the ship's manifest described them as "Negars." *Nigger* appeared thirty-two years earlier in 1587, a benign word when first used, possibly a corruption of either *Negro* or *Nigra,* neither considered an epithet. Negar? Negro? Nigra? Nigger? The latter was easier for many to pronounce. But who first corrupted the word — Caucasians or Negroes?

After 1964 thousands of Caucasians who used the word *nigger* were censured, persecuted, or lost their jobs. Until that year, Americans had a perfect right, and sometimes possibly even a sound reason, to pronounce words in their own way. But Negro appeasement recognized no boundaries. A prominent Caucasian television sportscaster was fired after referring to a Negro athlete as a "little monkey." And an attempt was made by a Pennsylvania university to expel a Caucasian student for using what was perceived as a racial slur, "water buffaloes," to describe noisy Negro students.

Corporations were easy prey for avaricious attorneys seeking "racial slurs." In 1996, a secretly taped conversation by a high-ranking oil company executive brought an end to a festering two-year-old discrimination complaint against the firm. The cowed corporation settled the lawsuit within days for an amount between 290 and 450 thousand gold ounces. The spine of the oil company turned to jelly when the recorded "black jelly beans" and "Nicholas" (sounds like *nigger*) was publicized.

No American English word or term is a safe haven from a racial slur designation. "Insensitive" behavior by ordinary and prominent Caucasians is punished more severely than are many felonies committed by Negroes. In 1988, when a Negro representative in the U.S. Congress accused hundreds of Caucasians of copulating with their mothers, he drew no denial from those so accused nor censure from anyone. At the same time, in St. Paul, Minnesota, one could legally burn the flag of the United States on the courthouse steps but committed a crime by burning a cross in one's own backyard.

By 1988, federal and state laws had cowed America's law-abiding, non-Negro population. Caucasians developed a fear of Negroes who would have their way and could not be controlled. Concerns for personal safety were justified, as Jared Taylor noted in 1992, "Though they are only 12 percent of the population, blacks commit more than half of all rapes and robberies and 60 percent of the murders in America." In 1995, one in three Negro men in their twenties was on probation, on parole, or incarcerated. This rate was approximately ten times the rate for Caucasian men of the same age.

Politically correct television stations colored, distorted, and shaded reporting and programming to downplay Negro problems. Jared Taylor wrote, "In real life, less than half of the people arrested for murder in the United States are white. In television dramas, 90 percent of the people arrested for murder are white." It was harder to control television news programs that graphically show brutal crimes committed by Negroes.

Relatives of Negro criminals increased exponentially, since few of these felons are orphans. It became nearly impossible to seat a Negro juror in a criminal trial who was not related by blood to someone with a felony conviction. (The prosecution rarely accepts a Caucasian as a juror in a criminal trial who has a blood relative who is a convicted felon.) Eyewitness accounts, deoxyribonucleic acid (DNA) evidence, even confessions played little part in many verdicts by juries that were chiefly Negro. Juries that were predominantly Negro, bonded by brotherhood, saw no evil, heard no evil, and spoke no evil when they delivered not-guilty verdicts for Negro defendants. Juries comprised mostly of Negroes slowed the Negro conviction rate in such urban environments as the New York City borough of the Bronx, where juries were more than 80 percent Negro and Hispanic. There, Negro defendants were acquitted in felony cases almost half of the time — nearly three times the national acquittal rate of 17 percent for all races. American laws were treated at best as incursions into Negro culture, at worst as racism.

The pendulum of justice for Negro criminals swung almost to the same wrongful apex to match the time when all-Caucasian juries refused to convict a Caucasian for bringing harm, even death, to a Negro. Almost nowhere were Negroes allowed to testify against Caucasians. But here the parallel ceases. At all times in American history, Caucasian juries convicted Caucasian criminals for wrongful actions against other Caucasians. Negro juries, however, increasingly freed Negro criminals regardless of whether the crime was committed against Caucasians or Negroes, although in the America of my time most Negro crime was directed against other Negroes.

Of course, the sorry course of political placation has escalated to your time, and the universe of Negro crime has expanded. At your presidency you found Negro criminal activity over ten times worse than when I write. Only you, America's Man on Horseback, can say *no* and mean it. Make lawbreakers of all shades of color into believers in your policies. You collected early payment of many criminals' debt to nature and relocated others to Africa and Siberia. When your *no* is fully believed, the majority of Negroes should become law-abiding citizens, just as they were before 1964.

The usual outcome of problem-solving is to restore to normalcy that which existed before the problem occurred. Your successes to date, however admirable, have only reestablished some peaceful portions of American life considered normal during the 1950s. Your problem-solving, however, does nothing to increase the ambition and intelligence of American Negroes.

Contemporary conservatives blame genes for the lower success levels of Negroes. Their liberal peers choose nutrition, environment, public education, discrimination, and a lack of self-esteem caused by slavery as responsible for the dilemma. Whatever reason, the broad-based lack of achievement and lower acumen remain for the overwhelming majority of Negroes worldwide.

You, America's Man on Horseback, can change dramatically the intellect and achievement of as many Negroes as you wish. Your predecessors also could have altered the equation but chose not to. (The dominant haves in power rarely share control with the nondominant have-nots. Power is shared only when sharing serves the purpose of the dominant — for example, when the breeding proclivities of the nondominant produce an overpowering numerical force.)

You inherited a decadent, dissolute, despairing America. You cannot, by edict, change the dominance and nondominance ratios among future American adults regardless of color. Appeals to the small percentage of dominant women to rear more children may go unheeded. A plea to nondominant women to withhold or quit delivering children will be ignored. Enforcement to keep births in check will fail as surely as did China's birthrate policy of 1979.

I appeal to your wisdom, your courage, and your love of the United States, Mr. President. An immense, generations-to-come benefit is yours to pluck from one of America's most serious problems. Turn countless American child tragedies into adult treasures. Initiate child-development schools on a scale the world has never seen. The finished products of the child-development schools will serve our nation greatly in times of peace and war. (Ironically, the output of privately funded Negro child-development schools of the same magnitude might well have halted the nation's decline and thus have prevented America's need for you.) Use to advantage the prolificacy of America's nondominant Negro population to seed this undertaking. Convert those offspring who are unwanted and abandoned into a mighty force of striving men and women of high intelligence to help restore our once-great nation.

CHAPTER SEVENTEEN

Child-Development School Successes

꩜

As you organize child-development schools to propel the United States to a new, better glory, turn again to history for lessons and guidelines.

Plato was one of the earliest Western thinkers who detailed the child-rearing methods that would achieve the goals he thought important. He recognized that what a child sees and hears early in life is as much a part of his education as is any formalized process; he knew that early experiences involving the interpretation of the moral beliefs of adults who are significant to the child influence the child's attitudes as an adult. Though taken out of the full context of the earliest utopia ever proposed in European literature, Plato's *Republic*, these excerpts present the flavor of his ideas on education.

What is this education to be, then? Perhaps we shall hardly invent a system better than the one which long experience has worked out, with its two branches for the cultivation of the mind and of the body. And I suppose we shall begin with the mind, before we start physical training.

Don't you understand, . . . that we begin by telling children stories, which, taken as a whole, are fiction, though they contain some truth? Such story-telling begins at an earlier age than physical training; that is why I said we should start with the mind.

And the beginning, as you know, is always the most important part, especially in dealing with anything young and tender. That is the time when the character is being moulded and easily takes any impress one may wish to stamp on it.

So far, then, as religion is concerned, we have settled what sorts of stories about the gods may, or may not, be told to children who are to hold heaven and their parents in reverence and to value good relations with one another.

Nor again must these men of ours be lovers of money, or ready to take bribes. . . .

Next, the upbringing of our young men must include physical training; and this must be no less carefully regulated throughout life from childhood onwards. In my view, which I should like you to consider, it is not true that a sound and healthy body is enough to produce a sound mind; while, on the contrary, the sound mind has power in itself to make the bodily condition as perfect as it can be. . . .

Plato maintained that both mind and body must be developed and disciplined, and that moral integrity can be instilled through religious training. He believed an effective educational system benefits a country and prevents the growth of lawlessness. Once an educational system proves its effectiveness and superiority in developing students to their greatest capacity, Plato asserted, the system must remain unchanging. He recognized that knowledge will continue growing and changing but believed that once a system demonstrates its practicality, it would be foolish to alter a proven process for the sake of change or variety. Plato designed his program for a group he termed the Guardians.

The rulers of the Ottoman Empire developed an educational system strikingly similar to that which Plato proposed for the education of the Guardians. No concrete proof exists that the Ottomans borrowed their ideas from him, but there is evidence that their rulers had great respect for Plato and his teachings. Plato divided the Guardians into Rulers (legislative) and Auxiliaries (executive);

the Ottomans differentiated between public officials and an elite military force.

The Ottoman system evolved some 1,700 years after Plato, around the time of the reign of Murad I (1360–1389). A new name surfaced in armed warfare, *Yeni Ceri* (new troops), or Janissaries, as the Europeans called them. Since Holy Law forbade the enslavement of fellow Muslims, Christian boys and young men were captured, converted to Islam, and made the sultan's slaves. They were extensively trained to serve the sultan. When a lull in the Ottomans' European conquests ended the flow of young Christian captives, a new source for recruits was found: the *devsirme* or levy of boys.

Every four or five years as needed, one thousand to three thousand boys were collected from the poor rural Christian sections of the sultan's regional possessions. Though it sounds cruel, many families welcomed this opportunity of advancement for a child. (Other Christians preferred converting to Islam rather than facing the sentimental and financial loss of a son.) Children were taken from near-poverty on drab farms and elevated to life in the palace, undergoing training to become public officials or members of the elite Janissary Corps. Strict measures were taken to keep out undesirables; those selected were judged for physical and mental aptitude, good moral fiber, and physical attractiveness. They came from the provinces, not the sophisticated cities; the idea was to obtain raw material that could be molded.

Although slaves, the children were educated in the sultan's palace schools (which were far superior to the Ottoman public schools) in Istanbul, Bursa, Edirne, and Galata. Mehmed II (the Conqueror) and Suleyman (the Magnificent) are credited with elevating the palace schools to remarkable heights as institutions for training superior military and administrative minds.

The students studied liberal arts as well as the arts and sciences of war and government, and they received rigorous physical training. Courses included calligraphy, music, architecture, painting, sculpture, history, mathematics, horsemanship, and weaponry. Pupils also learned a craft or trade. Future sultans underwent the same training.

Discipline and competition were intense. Those who excelled physically joined the Janissaries; those who showed superior mental capabilities continued training for civil and political careers. After years of schooling, the graduate was theoretically a scholar-athlete-gentleman and, most importantly, a sincere Muslim and devoted servant of the sultan.

No stigma was attached to royal slavery; the sultan himself had a slave mother. The *devsirme* system based promotion on merit alone. Each step on the way to power and success was earned. The captives were often treated as the sultan's adopted sons and brothers; they were his companions. These sons of ignorant farmers and herders formed a huge slave family and became rulers of an immense, powerful, and prosperous empire. They were allowed to own property, had many individual rights, and received lavish rewards for outstanding service. The rigid discipline and rich educational curriculum motivated them to achieve, and many made outstanding contributions to the Ottoman Empire. During the same period, their biological Christian brothers who remained with their parents followed and perpetuated the family's drab existence.

Initially, only men born into leading Muslim families held high positions such as grand vizier. By the time of the conquest of Istanbul, the *devsirme* had taken control; until the Empire's decline, the palace schools provided almost every court official, provincial governor, and military officer. Those in the highest positions were proud, not ashamed, of their humble beginnings. They believed the ability to succeed had nothing to do with birth; education and success were God's gifts to reward their zeal and hard work.

The Ottoman Empire began to decline after it reached its Age of Affluence; the end of the Age overlapped the Empire's Age of Decadence. Beginning with Suleyman, Turks with outside interests gained admittance to the Janissaries. The Janissaries married and enrolled their sons in the Corps, neither of which had previously been allowed. The levy of boys ceased, and the Janissaries deteriorated from a tightly disciplined, elite force of fifteen thousand to a self-perpetuating, pampered, and unruly guard of more than two hundred thousand.

Israel's kibbutz educational system also reflects the educational program Plato outlined in *The Republic*. The adult achievements of its students correspond with the adult successes of Ottoman palace students.

Zionist immigrants to Palestine founded the first kibbutz in 1909 at Degania on the Sea of Galilee. The movement's basic principle, then as now, is that set forth by Karl Marx: from each according to his abilities, to each according to his needs. Its structure is based on equality in all areas: work, housing, and child care. Even though the kibbutz embraces socialistic principles, it seems to function essentially as a democratic institution.

An estimated 270 kibbutzim contain about 3 percent of the country's population. By the mid-1980s, some one hundred thousand kibbutzniks were cultivating 42 percent of the available land and producing 50 percent of the country's agricultural output. Today high technology is replacing agriculture at many kibbutzim. Kibbutzim make half of Israel's industrial robots, produce solar-energy collectors used to heat Israeli homes, and even run hotels to take advantage of the tourist trade.

The kibbutz movement creates no waiting list for enrollment; quite the contrary. Even in the early days of the movement, the socialistic principles and communal existence proved too harsh for most. In 1921 a splinter group formed the moshav, a less-demanding experiment in collective living, in which homes and land are privately owned and farmers receive the profits from their labors. By the early 1980s, the moshavim had increased to about 350 with approximately 130 thousand members.

Contributions to Israel by individuals from the kibbutzim movement far exceed their small 3 percent population ratio. Of Israel's first six prime ministers, three came from the movement. About a third of all cabinet members between 1949 and 1967 were kibbutz members. During the Six Day War, 22 percent of the country's army officers and 30 percent of its air force pilots came from kibbutzim. Individuals from the kibbutzim are an elite. They enjoy good living conditions and can expect to secure the best jobs.

Perhaps the individual successes of kibbutzim members, disproportionately large in comparison to their small numbers and percentage of the population, lie in the dominance levels and child-rearing practices of the movement. The dominant members of the kibbutz share child care responsibilities along with equal sharing of all other tasks, thus influencing their young charges for dominance.

The kibbutz educational system was begun for practical and economic reasons, but over time ideology and education gained importance. The system was based on four major formulations. Kibbutzim allowed equality of the sexes. The kibbutz movement stood its best chance of self-perpetuation by educating children in special children's houses. Collective schooling was more scientific than leaving education in the hands of children's parents; children would be reared and trained by expert nurses and teachers, away from any family tensions. Lastly, a collective education would be more democratic than a traditional family education.

The system appears to have been strongly influenced by Sigmund Freud's ideas. It focuses on child management and discipline, the use of rewards and punishments, and a particular attitude toward the child's impulses and bodily desires and the attempt to sublimate them. No religious instruction is given.

The kibbutz takes responsibility for child rearing. Since kibbutzniks are not concerned with individual job remuneration, they can select child care personnel from among those best qualified to supervise, instruct, and discipline the children (corporal punishment is not used).

[CHAPTER EIGHTEEN]

Child-Development Schools for American Leadership

Now you embark upon the most audacious and important enterprise of your presidency; no person save you can shoulder such an undertaking. This bold push will equal or surpass all your successes of the next thirty years.

Create schools to develop the trailblazers necessary to nourish the American Empire. Use these schools to produce sufficient numbers of quality leaders for the United States to govern and administer the federal government and provide new troops to fill and command the armed forces. Grow your own vanguard to guide and protect the nation for generations to come.

Begin by using population percentages to divide the United States into geographical quadrants. Spread the schools equally, by population, among all states and locate them in rural rather than urban areas. For your future glory, name the child-development schools after yourself.

This endeavor is too important to entrust to one person. Select four superior, results-oriented individuals, one to head each sector. Choose young men and women with successful military backgrounds who exhibit outstanding management skills. Select those dedicated to you, your goals, and the task at hand. Do not consider educators. Few have had successful military careers and most, to my time, have been beaten down by federal and state mandates, school boards, teachers, teachers' unions, and parents of the incompetent. Encourage competition and innovation among the chosen four. Accept that some or all may fail and require replacement. Assure these leaders that less-than-expected results, with honest administration, are tolerable and that dishonesty, even with the appearance of success, is culpable.

Anticipate errors and transform early mistakes into future building blocks. Remember that nothing causes a great leader to be esteemed so much as great enterprises. The future potency of the American Empire could lie in this trailblazing endeavor.

Capitalize on the fecundity of America's nondominant Negro population for student enrollment; convert their undesired offspring into a mighty host to help restore the United States. Ask for, but do not take by force, unwanted healthy Negro children, who are dark in color, from birth (preferably) to age two. Sometime during the early years, a shortage of volunteered American Negro children may develop. In this event, extend the same offer to mothers in African countries to fill your enrollment. It is preferable that all African infants come from the eastern part of the continent, so as to vary appearances, and that they have dark- rather than light-colored skin.

As America's population could approximate 350 million at your time, start the program with 75,000 infants. By beginning with this small number, you will ease the concerns of intelligent, but bigoted, Caucasians who are frightened by the idea of a Negro elite. (Also advantageous is the belief, from years of propaganda, that such an experiment will fail.) Increase the number of infant enrollments by 20 percent per year, compounded to the needs of year ten for 386,000 new participants. After that, recruit only 300,000 new infants per year.

Select infant names from the ranks of those who shaped Western civilization. In addition, consider an enrollment of three boys to one girl. Men and women are equal as administrators, but you have more use in the military for men than for women. Of course, a more distant benefit to America lies in the children of the women graduates. Regardless of the dominance levels of the men they marry, dominant women are the ones who will rear dominant children. Dominant men graduates will not supply America with dominant offspring, as they tend to marry nondominant women, regardless of class, who in turn rear nondominant children.

When the first group nears graduation at year seventeen, some four million students will be enrolled in your child-development schools. This number equals that of the country's Negro slaves when the American Civil War began. The future accomplishments of these four million students stand to exceed the combined achievements, worldwide, of all Negroes ever born. Four million is enough; stop enrolling new students after that year. Phase out the child-development schools, one grade per year, until the last graduate. Even though the pool of nondominant Americans will start to grow again, the risk of too many dominant people focused on a single task is a greater hazard.

Draw teachers and other school personnel first from America's Midwest, which maintained traditional American values longer than other regions did. Their standard-accent speech presents an additional bonus to your elite children.

Furthermore, all surrogate mothers, teachers, and child-development school employees should be dominant, intelligent, disciplined, and committed totally to America's cause. They should be Caucasian and not obese. When you phase out the child-development schools, former surrogate mothers, teachers, and administrators will be in demand by private and public schools. The proven methods of your schools will have already been adopted by Americans to satisfy the country's renewed hunger for quality education.

Expect costs of 50 ounces of gold per child per year. Expenses will grow exponentially from the first-year expenditures of less than four million ounces of gold. In year ten almost two million children will be enrolled in your child-development schools with an estimated annual outlay of 100 million ounces of gold. This is a pittance compared to the government payouts of my time for welfare, dependent children, crime, incarceration, and such.

How or where else can you acquire a like amount of future good for an equal sum? You will need each and every enrollee to satisfy your towering ambitions for our great nation.

H A V E your four new groundbreaking leaders study analyses of the educational systems of Plato, the Ottomans, and the kibbutz of Israel. In addition, peruse offspring-rearing methods in the animal kingdom. Young animals imitate what they see: male dogs squat to urinate until they see another male dog raise his leg when urinating; ducks and killdeers use "broken wing" antics to lead predators away from their nests. These learned behaviors come from observation, not from instinct or teaching. Teachers in your schools must exhibit the achievement-oriented behavior you wish the children to learn. Do not stint, Mr. President; such teachers deserve remuneration of two to three times the average pay that schoolteachers of your time earn.

Chimpanzees, our nearest-of-kin primates, employ practices for rearing their young that are similar to those of humans. The male issue of dominant chimpanzee mothers become Alpha males of the group, just as male children of dominant human mothers become leaders in human society. As in human families, the offspring of nondominant chimpanzee mothers grow up to be followers, not leaders. The learned trait of dominance is observable, determinable, and consistent in both chimpanzee and human mothers. Future leaders are equally predictable in both species.

Similarly, in India young and uneducated men train baby elephants for a lifetime of work. The animals are disciplined and taught to work and not to kill. Thus, for a lifetime the elephant does not forget how to work and remembers "thou shall not kill."

Since 1964, a growing percentage of American mothers have failed to discipline and teach their children to work and not to kill. (Though these mothers would say that it is easier to train young elephants than their own unruly children.) Young mothers who want to rear their children well but were themselves reared poorly cannot do well — good intentions do not override ignorance. Further, the task seems not worth the time of these mothers, since politicians reward nonwork with welfare, just as judges and juries trying murder cases deliver verdicts of not guilty or probation or give light sentences. Nevertheless, Ayn Rand understood history when she wrote:

> At birth, a child's mind is tabula rasa; he has the potential of awareness — the mechanism of a human consciousness — but no content. Speaking metaphorically, he has a camera with an extremely sensitive, unexposed film (his conscious mind), and an extremely complex computer waiting to be programmed (his subconscious). Both are blank. He knows nothing of the external world. He faces an immense chaos which he must learn to perceive by means of the complex mechanism which he must learn to operate.
>
> If, in any two years of adult life, men could learn as much as an infant learns in his first two years, they would have the capacity of genius. To focus his eyes (which is not an innate, but an acquired skill), to perceive the things around him by integrating his sensations into percepts (which is not an innate, but an acquired skill), to coordinate his muscles for the task of crawling, then standing upright, then walking — and, ultimately, to grasp the process of concept-formation and learn to speak — these are some of an infant's tasks and achievements whose magnitude is not equaled by most men in the rest of their lives.

Knowing this, your child-development school leaders can learn much from Glenn Doman, an unsung American hero, a man of my time with rich thoughts. He offers inspired teaching ideas for surrogate mothers and teachers at your child-development schools. Among Glenn and Janet Doman's books are *How to Teach Your Baby to Read*, *How to Teach Your Baby Math*, *How to Give Your Baby Encyclopedic Knowledge*, *How to Multiply Your Baby's Intelligence*, and *How to Teach Your Baby to Be Physically Superb*.

Encouragement is not the same as permissiveness. Establish limits for behavior at an early age and require obedience. Have surrogate mothers and teachers stress the word *no* and compel compliance. *No* is the strongest word in the English language, and it rarely brings trouble to a person who uses it. *Yes* is the opposite, a word of appeasement, and its overuse ensures travail. *No* is easily reversed and then brings pleasure to the receiver. Reversing *yes* is difficult for the speaker and inevitably elicits anger from the receiver. Avoidance, as in the absence of a yes or no answer, is invariably construed to be *yes*. The absence of *no* creates for a child the illusion of life without behavioral boundaries, while the enforcement of *no* with infants and small children is the yeast of conscience.

The adult ability or inability to say *no* stems from childhood training. As children, they were or were not taught the word: the obedient learned *no*, the disobedient did not. Other than entertainers and politicians, society rewards most those who can say *no* with ease; those who cannot rarely become great surgeons, top executives, or victorious military commanders.

The child who by age five learns the alphabet and reads and writes cannot become illiterate. Some contend that dyslexia derives from a faulty gene. There are those who say that no child with dyslexia can read and write by age five. Prove them wrong. It will appear that early teaching deactivates the gene causing dyslexia. Also, pronunciation, accent, diction, and grammar are imitated by the young. A child of any ethnicity can learn advanced mathematics and several languages with the same ease that he learns bad grammar and improper pronunciation. Early demands for mental excellence, if started at infancy, produce mental giants. But this is not enough.

At the age that understanding develops, teach the children first to believe, then know, that they are elite, second to none worldwide, save you. Teach them that their purpose in life is to serve their country. Instill in these children the knowledge that they are unique and superior to others. At the same time, train them to have sympathy, but not pity, for other Americans. Imprint personality and purpose in their minds at this tender age. Early physical control is equally important. Your schools can deliver all this plus more.

When demands are made for early childhood accomplishment, the child naturally develops a fear of failure. A child's fear of failure becomes an adult phobia. High achievement is just one of many psychological needs set in place by making early demands for childhood excellence. Expanding the number and magnitude of adult successes then becomes a way of life to assuage the phobia of failure. Another example, demands for energetic behavior and punishment of sloth will create a childhood fear of being lethargic that becomes an adult phobia. Energetic behavior then contributes to accomplishment and alleviates the phobia of indolence.

After determining that all demands for childhood achievement set by the child-development schools are capable of being met, do not rationalize or accept failure. Further, at each stage of growth, praise and reward the child's mental and physical accomplishments and, when deserved, administer corporal punishment.

There is a published average for normal childhood achievements in America. Without exception, your charges should accomplish the average when they are at least 30 percent younger. In my time, fourteen months is the average age when infants walk. If this remains the same in your day, encourage and expect your school-children to walk before ten months.

The age range of infants taught to achieve daytime continence varies widely as I write. Toilet training at an early age is a major indicator of adult achievement. Loving mothers with high expectations of their children complete the child's toilet training before or by age twenty-four months. Only 26 percent of American infants have these special mothers, while mothers with less expectations for achievement represent the majority, 59 percent, and take thirty months to conclude toilet training. Thirteen percent of American mothers have minimal expectations for childhood accomplishments and disregard the soiled child for thirty-six months. These shameless mothers are joined by another two percent of mothers who forgo toilet training for over thirty-six months, leaving the child to train himself. Set the goal for toilet training your school-children at twenty-one months.

The children in your child-development schools can achieve a 30-percent or better reduction from the average achievement times for infant, child, and adolescent mental and physical performances. This alone ensures success for your child-development program and opens new and exciting vistas for achievement possibilities.

Child-rearing practices in America will evolve over time to conform to the boundaries you set for adult behavior, Mr. President. However, current turbulent conditions deny you the luxury of waiting for such change. Therefore, design the curriculum of your child-development schools to fit your unique period.

Teach the children of your schools to kill, without remorse, when so directed. All living beings owe a debt to nature, and your students will make the enemies of America pay their debt early. Accept only valor and honor; avoid cowardice and dishonor at all costs. At the same time, infuse your pupils with a sense of justice and fairness, which are on a par with valor and honor. Teach them reverence for God and love for you, the tool of God. Hard work combined with physical and mental accomplishments becomes a way of life for your schoolchildren.

Each pupil from your child-development schools owes his allegiance to you, to his group, and to God. The Caucasian Janissaries and public officeholders of the Ottoman Empire would give their lives for the Sultan and their student group. Your Negro counterparts will do no less, Mr. President; that you are Caucasian and they are Negro matters not.

Murad I chose Caucasian male children to become the feared Janissaries and brilliant administrators of the Ottoman Empire a century before Columbus discovered America. The selection of boys stemmed from religious beliefs. Since the Muslim religion forbade the enslavement of other Muslims, the boys happened to be Christian and Caucasian. The result was an elite light-skinned force, fierce and intelligent, amid a darker population. This is little different from what you will have, only reversed. Now you see the merit of enrolling only dark-skinned Negroes in the child-development schools. Because of their color, this group will not truly fit with Caucasian Americans, even those few Caucasians who match their intelligence. Centuries of color separation, by force or by choice, preclude large-scale fraternization.

The graduates from your schools will have little in common with almost all Negroes of your day, since few common denominators will exist between your graduates and other American Negroes. Differences in intellect, work ethic, and speech cannot be bridged by color alone. Your graduates will have no regard for those who will not work and little respect for those who labor only from necessity. In my time, Caucasians who did not work but did steal were called "white trash." It is altogether possible that your graduates will add the term "black trash" to describe Negroes who steal and do not work. Look for American Negroes, the Caucasian population, and all ethnic groups to respect, and even fear, your charges; their color combined with their intelligence and accomplishments will be most intimidating.

Schoolchildren are impressed by visits and speeches from prominent personages. From 1964 forward, public schools paraded a variety of "celebrities" for the impression of young minds. Among those important visitors were actors, sports figures, popular musicians, politicians, and prison inmates. Invite none of these to your schools. Bring renowned scientists to talk about the splendors of science. Skilled physicians can speak of the personal gratification of saving lives. Fierce captains and colonels can recount tales of heroes, of valor, of the taking of lives in defense of the nation, and of not fearing to die for one's country.

The loss of the dominance trait to your time will be most evident in a shortage of high achievers, particularly in the fields of engineering, mathematics, and medicine. A significant number of your graduates will qualify for and be interested in specialized fields among these categories. Enroll them, at government expense, in superior universities of their choice. Further, when your students graduate from the child-development schools, enlist the majority into America's military. Utilize the government facilities at the Air Force Academy, the Naval Academy, and the Military Academy to further educate the brightest of your elite.

Reflect on the accomplishments, integrity, and valor of Brigadier General Benjamin O. Davis, Sr.; Lieutenant General Benjamin O. Davis, Jr.; General Roscoe Robinson, Jr.; Vice Admiral Samuel L. Gravely, Jr.; Brigadier General Frank E. Peterson, Jr.; and General Colin L. Powell. These heroic American warriors brought honor to the nation and to their splendid mothers. One thousand such men-at-arms from your schools? Nay, look forward to a half million — or more!

CHAPTER NINETEEN

Sins of the Fathers

Your resolution of lawlessness in the United States was dazzling. Your crime agenda successfully addressed the demand side of illegal drug use, making the game not worth the candle. Where is America's gratitude?

Rebirthing the American work ethic was a splendid accomplishment that no one save you could have achieved. Stopping the spread of *Slim* by quarantine saved countless American lives. Ridding the country of legal gambling set America on a moral course. Punishing the past purveyors of dishonesty in government and bringing about a more honest government was a rare achievement. Your child-development schools will provide domestic protection for citizens, honest government administration, and future security from foreign conquest. Time after time you did the right thing for our nation. Where is America's gratitude?

Under your leadership, Mr. President, the country is on a plateau and will either climb further or begin to decline. Your magnificent achievements to date bring glory to you and to your country, but with a hidden cost. As Harvey Mackay so aptly stated, "Gratitude is the least deeply felt of all human emotions. . . . Hatred and even love endure, but there is in the human makeup that which is unwilling to bear the burden of being grateful, and therefore morally beholden to anyone for very long." Ingratitude and its companion, resentment, flourish. You gave much — in your zeal, perhaps too much. The peace and quiet you gave the nation allow your enemies time to multiply a thousandfold. The wicked rest not and take advantage of any breathing spell to pull you down.

By nature you are a loner with much power but few friends. Your achievements are due to your will and leadership, not to alliances created or friendships built. Your enemies will capitalize on this combined virtue and flaw. The populace, secure now, is vulnerable to troublemakers who agitate to bring back sweet portions of the Age of Decadence while contending that the nation can retain the beneficial aspects of your efforts. Neither the proposal's lack of substance nor the impossibility of delivering its promise diminishes the message. However, people listen and will begin public protests. You need no public turmoil brought against you now. Nothing should distract you from your most important task: presiding over America's rebirth.

You have the support of domestic law enforcement agencies, judges, a plethora of government services, and the military. But do not use these entities to quell protests and demonstrations or for purges. If you suppress the people, you will be, at best, a dictator. Americans have heard lies from too many for too long. They no longer give their faith freely; trust must be earned. You need time to gain the unswerving trust and goodwill of the people. You need still greater successes to bond the general populace to you.

Your real enemies are a special and elite group. Greed and needs for control and power propel them into treacherous games to dispose of you and all the good you may do in the future. But you are in command, and they cannot push you out as their British counterparts did Prime Minister Winston Churchill, whose leadership during World War II saved Great Britain. His reward? He was forced from office.

Your adversaries are protected by their wealth and position from the vulgar and from the likes of you. Such groups bob and weave throughout history, pulling down kings and reformers alike. They provide the money and motion to foment civil unrest and have the wealth to buy their way out of trouble. Most are physical cowards at heart and abhor delivering violence personally. They exhibit prudence and self-control, preferring to pull strings from a distance. Adroit at manipulation, they thrive on sending and receiving "signals."

As you remedied America's ills one by one, group by group, it was inevitable that you would clash with this sheltered clique of dissatisfied power brokers. This protected genus of greed is without peer among avaricious Americans. They have no fear of your laws, having already begun bribing your judges and circumventing the law without penalty. Their money and position shield them from you so completely that you cannot see what they are doing.

They are not like America's ignorant-lawless, the first and easiest group you defeated. This advantaged assemblage not only hates you, but they can undo you. They love themselves first, last, and most of all. Any love that they let spill over, after they have drunk their fill, trickles down to close family, but none dribbles onto our nation or its welfare. You are at war with real adversaries wanting to overthrow you. These moneyed elitists fear neither God nor you. Their envy of your power blinds them to potential danger, and they lend a deaf ear to your summons for patriotism. Political murder is the last resort to cure individual deafness, but even that does little to heal group blindness.

Your successes to date have served to hold in check a possible second civil war with 1861 boundaries but have not eliminated racial hatred. Add to this ethnic and religious differences going back two centuries. Your adversaries will attempt to foment this below-the-surface tension into an erupting volcano.

I know, Mr. President, that you have considered using terror to serve your purposes, as have both puny and great leaders before you. This crossroad is only one of many from which you must choose the correct route; a wrong selection here could make it your last.

Sifting through history's accounts of how other leaders resolved similar problems, your choices appear limitless. Should you loosen your grip on the forces that maintain law and order, a second civil war could materialize, costing hundreds of thousands, perhaps millions, of lives before you choose sides and end the war. You could provoke a class war or turn the majority into a force to eradicate a minority group, or vice versa. You could select ethnic groups as scapegoats on which to focus hatred and violence. In any case, your adversaries, regardless of the side they choose, could be disposed of during the ensuing turmoil.

There should be better ways to resolve trying problems. Maximum coercion is easy to start but hard to contain. A reign of terror too often develops a life of its own, not unlike the spread of infectious bacteria and malignant viruses. Initiators of widespread terror many times become infected themselves, as did Maximilien Robespierre in 1794. China's last ten-generation epoch ended in 1911. Near the end of that cycle, the Taiping Rebellion — the bloodiest civil war in recorded history — left twenty-five million people dead.

I am against terrorism in any form or fashion. Do not employ terror as a means to an end. It is not the American way. Remember, your goal is to rebuild America, then surpass its former glory. Unleashing terror may well destroy the very people you wish to save. Exercise self-control, as the claim of Machiavelli that "neither conscience nor infamy should dismay you because those who win, in whatever mode they win, never receive shame from it" is false. Acts of infamy destroy the moral character of the individual and the respect of others.

Still, having said this, I believe full well that you will disregard me and pursue this harsh course. I fear for our nation. It is a terrible thing that America has been brought to such a pass. You, like other leaders before you, are contemplating this extreme solution as your enemies leave you few options.

Believing that America is destined to suffer a time of terror at your hands, I offer the following to limit the number stricken. This could be a way to achieve the effects of terror, as it is conventionally recognized, and yet allow you to minimize the loss of life and prevent it from escalating to wholesale slaughter. As much as possible, avoid injustice, divisiveness, loss of independence, and the deaths of large numbers of the general population. It is only that elite group of power brokers that you need to silence.

History shows that nations can adapt to predictable acts of terrorism. It is random terror practiced indiscriminately against citizens from all stations of life that produces such paralyzing anxiety that tears the whole society apart. Perhaps the Bible provides an old way to combine both random terror and predictability to bring

Hell to earth for a few from the most monied and powerful elite without the taking of millions of lives.

> The Bible takes sin in dead seriousness. Unlike many modern religionists, who seek to find excuses for sin and to explain away its seriousness, most of the writers of the Bible had a keen awareness of its heinousness, culpability, and tragedy. They looked upon it as no less than a condition of dreadful estrangement from God, the sole source of well-being.
>
> [*The Interpreter's Dictionary of the Bible:* sin, sinners]

*

I the Lord thy God am a jealous God, visiting the iniquity of the fathers upon the children unto the third and fourth generation of them that hate me.
[EXOD. 20:5; 34:7; DEUT. 5:9]

*

In the iniquities of their fathers shall they pine away.
[LEV. 26:39]

*

Prepare slaughter for his children for the iniquity of their fathers.
[ISA. 14:21]

*

Our fathers have sinned, and are not; and we have borne their iniquities.
[LAM. 5:7]

*

They are turned back to the iniquities of their forefathers.
[JER. 11:10]

*

An important consideration is the distinction between corporate and individual responsibility for sin. In its early development Israel was very much influenced by a dynamistic concept of corporate guilt, as strikingly appears in the account of Achan's punishment (Josh. 7). Not only was the guilty man put to death, but all his goods, his flocks, and his family also perished with him (vs. 24). The family group was a much more significant entity than the individual person. When the head of such a group transgressed, he transmitted guilt to every member of it (cf. II Sam. 21:6; II Kings 9:8; etc.).

Even in official Yahwism this conception played an important role. In the great Covenant formulations, however, its scope was somewhat restricted. Thus, according to the Decalogue (Exod. 20:5; Deut. 5:9; cf. Exod. 34:7; Num. 14:18), the iniquity of the fathers is to be visited upon the children, but only "to the third and fourth generation."

[*The Interpreter's Dictionary of the Bible:* sin, sinners]

*

That a man is requited for his own deeds is a theme of the earliest sources. He is not, however, conceived of as an isolated entity, but as inextricably bound up with his family, tribe, people, city, and land. And since his life extends in effect beyond his own person, the scope of his reward and punishment may also.

[*The Religion of Israel,* Yehezkel Kaufmann, trans. and abr. Moshe Greenberg]

*

The scope of collective responsibility before God might extend even to a large group, a city or kingdom.

[*The Religion of Israel*]

*

R. Jose b. Hanina said that Moses made four declarations [*gezerot*], and then four prophets came after him and annulled them. Of these four, the fourth was Ezekiel, for whereas Moses said, "He visits the sins of the fathers upon the children" (Exod. XX, 5), Ezekiel came and annulled the assertion, even as it says, "The soul that sins, that soul [alone] shall die" (Ezek. XVIII, 20).

[*A Rabbinic Anthology,* eds. C. G. Montefiore and H. Loewe]

These quotes from the Bible and religious scholars are arranged out of context to present the development of *tingere,* a legal concept rooted in the Bible, later termed *attaynder, atteindor, attendre, attaindour,* and *attender.* "Attainder," "corruption of blood," and "pains and penalties" are contemporary terms developed over time from the biblical punishment for sins of the father.

While the Bible may inspire your actions, do not say so. Citing a source to bolster your actions weakens the strength of a decision already made. Hold yourself above reconciling religious issues, quoting the Bible to muster support, and being drawn into religious debate. You are the author and the authority for your decisions and will rise or fall by your actions.

Voices praised you at your ascendancy, Mr. President, and you received public encouragement to find and punish frauds among the citizens. Petitioners begged you to accept their lists of those who had wronged them and their families. Blood debts created in the ninth and tenth generations cried out for payment. To avoid the excesses of past liberators, such as Mao Tse-tung, you refused to accept liquidation lists from the vengeful. Should you be bent on abominable actions, now could be the time, though belated, to address those initial pleas for vengeance. Respond in a different fashion from what was advocated by the many petitioners with their long lists.

History could record that America's Man on Horseback was a great leader with a strong moral character, was merciful and gracious, slow to anger, and abounding in steadfast love for and faithfulness to his country. While he kept steadfast his love for the nation's millions, and forgave iniquity and transgression, he would not clear the transgressors nor allow their descendants to profit from their detrimental and abusive actions, visiting the iniquity of the fathers upon the children and the children's children to the third and fourth generation.

CHAPTER TWENTY

Accountability for the Past

❧

The great majority of humans live only for today, for now. The present quickly becomes the past. Personal accountability for words and actions disappears with every setting sun. Those who bring up the past and expect accountability for past actions are accused of not playing fairly the game of Living for Today Only.

Your elitist enemies reason the same way. Hell strikes no fear in their hearts or minds. They view God as forgiving, little different from the parole boards, judges, and juries in the years before your presidency. Your moneyed adversaries feel secure that Heaven awaits those who repent, even those who committed great evil. So they say. In truth, they believe in neither Heaven nor Hell. Without conscience, they spend their lives making sure that they are not shorted at the table-of-thieves banquets. Death, while freeing them from all sorrow and pain, also frees them of accountability for their past unconscionable acts.

These deceased, however, can still be made accountable for the deeds they committed while alive. In showing the living at your time the earthly hell that you can deliver to their descendants, even the wiliest adversaries conspiring against you can be given just cause to rethink the probable outgrowth of their actions. Let them see that retribution can come even after they themselves have departed this world.

You can decree unique Laws of Attainder and Corruption of Blood, giving you, and you alone, the legal right to punish, without trial and without a proclamation of guilt, the living for the sins of their fathers, their grandfathers, their great-grandfathers, and even their great-great-grandfathers. (These decrees would apply also to the original person, if living.) These two edicts allow you to visit the iniquity of the father upon the children and upon the children's children unto the third and fourth generation.

The United States Constitution prohibits such power in Article 3, Section 3, where it forbids bills of attainder and corruption of blood. The framers of the Constitution were particularly troubled with legislative attainder and the ex post facto law. Article 1 explicitly enjoins Congress and the states from exercising either of them.

An ex post facto law renders an act punishable even if the act was not punishable when it was committed. Ex post facto provides for a penalty when none existed at the time the act was committed, or it increases the penalty. Such laws obviously offend one's sense of regularity; they are clearly arbitrary. Indeed, even without the specific constitutional prohibition, a legislative enactment purporting to penalize particular conduct committed before the act is passed would undoubtedly run afoul of the Due Process Clause.

But you suspended the old Constitution, due process and all. At a later and less perilous time, reincorporate the laws against attainder, corruption of blood, and ex post facto. Reinstate due process in a new Constitution, for under most conditions these are important limits to ensure justice and prevent arbitrary tyranny.

For centuries, kings, emperors, and dictators alike used *tingere*, with adaptations and language changes, to maintain power and punish enemies. Eradication of entire families made real the threat of future use of this direst of punishments. For thirty years, during the Wars of the Roses (1455–1485), the royal houses of Lancaster and York both used *attaynderes* indiscriminately.

Stalin added a new twist to this age-old tool of terror. He gave his high-level, mostly imagined enemies a choice: confess guilt for all criminal charges in open court or watch as every living forbear, family member, and descendant was eliminated. Regardless of his choice, the victim-enemy knew that he was doomed. Stalin's show trials were immensely successful. The accused confessed whole-heartedly to staggering crimes against the Soviet Union. All were found guilty and executed. Stalin kept his word and spared the families of the accused conspirators; this act of kindness quickened confessions from the newly accused. (Stalin was not devoid of humor. He periodically included the name of his most ardent supporter, Molotov, on extermination lists. When this happened, other politburo members avoided Molotov as if he carried a communicable disease. Only after Molotov's health became endangered by terror-driven diarrhea would Stalin end his cat-and-mouse game.) The show trials finally ran their course — not because of rebellion, but after entire segments of industry and government faltered. Not many managers were left to run the railroads and factories, and too few physicians remained to treat the ill.

In Iraq, Saddam Hussein delivered less subtlety and more brutality to his adversaries. Each countryman-enemy was executed simultaneously with every living ancestor, family member, descendant, and in-law. No future seeds could sprout; the entire lineage ceased to exist, forever.

Adolf Hitler directed his brand of attainder and corruption of blood based on the bloodlines of those with "tainted blood." Gypsies qualified, as did all whose blood was "tainted" by at least one Jewish ancestor. Hitler elevated and punished corruption of blood on a scale heretofore unknown. The outcome of World War II could have differed if Hitler had cultivated, embraced, and then rewarded Germany's Jewish minority of 600,000 for efforts on his behalf, rather than ultimately murdering one-third of the world's 18 million Jews.

In the centuries before Hitler, common folk had little fear of attainder and corruption of blood. The privileged used these tools of terror against their peers, the nobility and upper classes. Reducing the number in a family to zero ensured that no one was left to inherit titular rights, power, castles, and lands, since power bases were inherited rather than earned. The high and mighty feared attainder and corruption of blood more than any horror this world or the next had to offer, while working people delighted to see the great brought down.

When corruption of blood is invoked and brings about the demise of one thousand innocents, ten million will shiver. Again, I beseech you, Mr. President. Do not make middle-class Americans shiver; they are not part of such hand-me-down wealth, power, or position. Do not inflict terror on the middle class or the working poor, for they are the ones who want most to be your friends.

Absolute edicts of attainder and corruption of blood place the Shangfang sword in your hands. How will you use it? How much and how often you employ it partially determines the outcome. If used as a symbol only, the Shangfang sword is a transparent and empty threat. Worst of all is its overuse, for this ensures that, in time, the sword will reverse direction and come at you.

Attainder and corruption of blood could be used selectively, rather than promiscuously, to send a signal to heretofore untouchable adversaries. The middle class and poor should, as in earlier times, remain unaffected. Make sure, Mr. President, that your actions are always on behalf of America and never to serve personal revenge, for, according to Walter Scott, "Vengeance is the sweetest morsel to the mouth that ever was cooked in hell!"

A contemporary attainder and corruption of blood list prepared by one of your trusted advisers has drawbacks. Those of your time will be hard-pressed to be objective in selecting contemporary wrongdoers and their descendants. They will be tempted to select living enemies and work backward, instigating revenge rather than random terror. In addition, the selectees may not have enough living descendants to invoke three to four generations of reckoning. A list of your time, regardless of source, would not free you from subjectivity and would smack of revenge.

Again, I say, do not pursue terror. That you fail to heed me is expected. Even so, for the sake of our great nation, I will continue to assist you, if I can. You are America's president and commander in chief; it is not my place to sit in judgment of you. If you are determined to follow this dreadful course, there may be merit in considering an attainture list from an earlier time. Books, magazines, and newspaper accounts, along with court documents and congressional records, can be researched to help you determine what is or is not a quality list.

Many leaders born in the seventh and eighth generations

brought varying degrees of intentional and unintentional harm to America during the ninth and tenth generations. More than a few cared little about the suffering their deeds brought to thousands of other Americans, their children, and their children's children. Many of these power brokers concerned themselves first with feathering their personal nest; next with leaving considerable money, position, and power to their offspring; and finally with perpetuating these advantages for their seed for generations to come.

If determined to pursue this dreadful course, you can save many American lives and still effect your purpose with a short attainder and corruption of blood list. It need cover only leaders in fields of enterprise from my time. It is their descendants who are most likely to move in the same circle with the puppet masters of your time: corporate (particularly insurance), media, and stock market leaders; attorneys; and professional politicians (but ignore former presidents, as they were elected by the majority of American voters).

Since those selected to depart this world are relatively few in number, the military need not be involved; instead, a special services branch of national security could efficiently and speedily handle the proscription task. The assets of those cleansed can be sold without fanfare through the Internal Revenue Service with the proceeds going to the United States Treasury.

A one-time, quick action should bring about the intended results. (Even though the general populace is fascinated by "enemies lists," do not promulgate a list; that only wastes time and indicates weakness. Most recognize the distinction between words and deeds. Public hearings by Senator Joseph McCarthy accomplished little more than the ruin of a few reputations, including his own; and President Richard Nixon's "enemies list" was a paper tiger.) A clear signal to those moneyed and powerful men of your time would be given and received, for the affected descendants will be members of the elite of your time. Many will be innocent friends and acquaintances of your enemies, if not your enemies in their own right. Attainder and corruption of blood recognize no innocents. For the first time in American history, citizens will perish without a trial and, even, without a pronouncement of guilt.

Remember, it is not that specific sins against the country are being punished or even that those sins committed would be punished if they were committed again. The direst dread of selective attainder and corruption of blood when making the selection from a generation or more ago is that it affects the high and mighty of your time randomly and appears to lend itself to expansion.

Expect the seriousness of your action and the ensuing shock to silence your adversaries for years. However, this action will not go unnoticed. If your effort is in vain, your enemies will attempt to turn public revulsion into national hatred of you. Should your first exercise of this tool fail, do not expand or repeat it, and do not let that decision be known. Instead, should more severity be needed, select another method and, again, make an effort to hold down the number of victims.

Limit your search through the past to Caucasian Americans. Investigating Hispanic, Negro, and Oriental Americans is time wasted. Although some committed heinous crimes, pay them no mind. Even if many would have inflicted damage to the nation had they had the opportunity, few were in a position to do so since they never belonged to America's elite.

Sift through lists of past members of the establishment for likely candidates. Do not rule out those who enjoyed honor and preeminence; the most skilled scoundrels hide among the illustrious. Discard the names of those wretches associated with public insults. Open ridicule alone makes them unworthy of your time.

One such doleful case was Joseph R. Biden, Jr., a U.S. senator. In mid-1987, Neil Kinnock, the British Labour party leader, asked, "Why am I the first Kinnock in a thousand generations to be able to get to university? . . . Was it because all our predecessors were thick?" In several speeches later that year, Senator Biden recited, "Why is it that Joe Biden is the first ever to go to a university? . . . Is it because I'm the first Biden in a thousand generations to get a college and a graduate degree that I was smarter than the rest?" Senator Biden's presidential chances evaporated after being accused of plagiarizing Kinnock's speech. The media made much of the theft but was kind to Senator Biden about stealing the phrase "a thousand generations." That lack of logic was never publicized. In 1987 the American Civil War had occurred barely five generations ago. Just thirty-one generations had gone by since Genghis Khan conquered China and English barons forced King John to sign the Magna Carta. Less than eighty generations ago Jesus Christ was born. The first stone wall was built around the world's first city, Jericho, no more than four hundred generations ago. Neil Kinnock foolishly passed off that he traced the education of his ancestors going back to 23,000 B.C., the era of Cro-Magnon man. A thousand generations? Biden, even less bright than Kinnock, stole fool's gold.

Another ridiculed rascal, Senator Edward M. Kennedy, met his mother's poor expectations for him. He achieved little in his lifetime, neither good nor bad. He wronged a friend, his family, and himself, but he caused little injury to other Americans.

Mr. President, pity and pass over Senators Biden and Kennedy and others of their made-sport-of stripe. Look elsewhere for scoundrels. A motherlode of heretofore undisclosed details of criminal activities awaits you. Clever crooks, compliant judges, and friendly prosecutors united to exploit the advantages of court-ordered sealed documents. This tool kept secret the specifics of financial crimes, which penalized primarily the middle class.

Beginning in the 1980s, sophisticated crime ran rampant. White-collar criminals, for example, raped the savings and loan industry, costing the federal government a loss of 1.2 billion gold ounces. Since this sum was equal to four and a half times the nation's entire gold holdings, politicians covered the theft by raising taxes and by selling additional government bonds.

Among the hundreds of prosecutions, one was unique at the time in size, scope, and number of individuals involved. On March 2, 1992, the Office of Thrift Supervision filed administrative charges in Washington, D.C., seeking an unprecedented monetary sum from Kaye, Scholer, Fierman, Hays and Handler, a prestigious New York law firm employing about 390 lawyers. In addition, federal regulators sought to freeze the assets of Kaye, Scholer and, further, to bar it from practicing banking law.

Approximately two years before, Kaye, Scholer had agreed to pay the equivalent of 52,139 gold ounces to settle a civil lawsuit filed against it and others by the bondholders of American Continental. The suit alleged that American Continental bondholders were defrauded as a result of false financial statements, which the thrift issued, and that Kaye, Scholer bore some responsibility. The firm did not admit any wrongdoing, and the bill was covered by insurance.

With the new action of March 1992, federal regulators demanded damages equal to 675,000 gold ounces for allegedly misleading regulators about the true financial state of Lincoln Savings and Loan Association. Kaye, Scholer's client, Charles H. Keating, Jr., headed American Continental, which, in turn, controlled Lincoln Savings. In less than a week, and without a trial, Kaye, Scholer settled for a reduced fine equal to only 100,000 gold ounces, and no partner went to prison. According to newspaper accounts, about half the fine was covered by the firm's insurance (National Union Fire Insurance Company was among the insurance companies involved), and the remainder was to be paid by 110 partners over four years. More specifically, the government's Temporary Order to Cease and Desist made a special reference to withholding 25 percent of the earnings of those who were partners in the law firm as of December 1, 1987.

However, according to the *Martindale-Hubbell Law Directory,* eighty-nine men and women appeared to be partners of Kaye, Scholer, Fierman, Hays and Handler as of December 1, 1987. Adding to the confusion, the Office of Thrift Supervision's news release on March 8, 1992, noted that "a significant majority of partners in the law firm, including members of its Banking Practice Group, were without involvement in the acts that led to the OTS charges." This statement alone gives notice that a list of Kaye, Scholer's partners as of December 1, 1987, would be worthless.

Still, who paid the uninsured remainder? Some portion must have been funded by three attorneys singled out for additional agreed-to punishment, the respondents Peter M. Fishbein, Karen E. Katzman, and Lynn Toby Fisher. The law firm's capitulation was well publicized, but who was scheduled to pay what portion of the fine was not.

It appears that records of the final settlement with the firm, which possibly included the names involved and amounts to be paid, were sealed from public scrutiny. Sealed documents serve but one purpose — concealment of the guilty. Mr. President, nothing can be sealed from your eyes. Break each seal and make public every secret document in America to your time. *Un*deceive Americans — let the public see the corporate and financial chicanery that American judges suppressed.

Assuredly more worthy lawyer-elite can be found. Look over Jones, Day, Reavis and Pogue, a prominent law firm of my time. They also involved themselves in the thrift industry debacle, perhaps doing more harm than Kaye, Scholer. Committing similar offenses and following Kaye, Scholer's lead, the law firm of Jones, Day, Reavis and Pogue avoided trial, partner incarceration, and a large monetary fine. They too beat down government agents to a lesser sum.

I present names of individuals from my time who may have brought harm, in varying degrees, knowingly or unknowingly, to the United States of America or to other Americans. I assure you this is not a quality list; without doubt many Americans of my time could compose a far superior list. Consider this roster only as an outline around which to plan your future slate, not as a list from which to select names. I want no grief to come to these individuals, if alive, or their descendants. This cross section may or may not guide you in preparing a comparable list. Perhaps seeing the abhorrent enormity of decrees of attainder and corruption of blood will serve as a deterrent against terror of any sort.

I prefer to avoid voluminous newspaper quotes, legal jargon, and lecturing about misdeeds. Perhaps rhyme can accomplish the same — and quicker. As an example, consider the banking scandals of the 1980s.

> *Many unwise loans they took,*
> *To enlarge their size, increase their book.*
> *Government lawyers, their accountants as well,*
> *Didn't stop the fraud, just ignored the smell.*
>
> *The public doesn't realize,*
> *That "Insured Accounts" are at best a guise,*
> *And, if banks fail, then it is they*
> *Who, to bail them out, must pay and pay.*

Our nation's insurance institutions "protect" their policy holders against loss.

> *Insurance companies with a need*
> *To line their pockets, feed their greed.*

Investment bankers deserve a mention.

> *Now, here's a group of stand-up guys,*
> *Who've worked their skills before your eyes —*
> *Ivan Boesky, Marty Siegel,*
> *Boyd L. Jefferies, is he regal!*
> *And the "Roberts," Freeman, Chestman,*
> *Never knew which one's the "Best Man."*
> *Edward J. DeBartolo, Sr.*
> *Among these he ranks at least "monsignor."*
> *Paul Bilzerian, David Sofer,*
> *Can't call either one a loafer!*
> *Nahum Vaskevitch, Timothy Tabor,*
> *Earn great fruits for their hard labor.*
> *And, John Mulheren, Jr., will,*
> *Like Bruce L. Newberg, fill the bill.*
> *Richard Wigton, Lowell J. Milken,*
> *James T. Sherwin, all are silken.*
>
> *Plus, some firms that are well-known,*
> *You can see how big they've grown —*
> *Kidder Peabody, Goldman Sachs,*
> *Realize changes, won't relax.*
> *Princeton Newport Partners, too,*
> *Merrill Lynch, you ask, they do.*
> *And Drexel Burnham Lambert shines*
> *At helping folks meet bottom lines.*

Back to insurance firms, lest they be forgotten and never brought to mind.

> *Insurance companies, in their way,*
> *Created equal harm;*

While claiming fair dealing day by day,
Self-preservation was their alarm.
They charged customers overmuch,
And failed to pay just claims,
Owned politicians they could "touch,"
Weren't accountable for their aims.
They saw all Americans as equal prey,
No matter what their state;
Insured or not, folks had to pay
Collection lawyers, and then wait.

American International Group is one of these,
"Mo" Greenberg is its chief,
Sells the most commercial insurance, if you please,
Also, fields the utmost grief.
But, law firms' claims are quickly paid —
AIG sees advantage there —
Other contracted claims are just delayed,
The distinction seems unfair.

And the State Farm Group we note as well,
No "farmers" in this band,
Personal auto and homeowners insurance they sell
Is the largest in the land.
Edward B. Rust, Jr. is their CEO,
And heads eight of their product lines;
"Pay slowly," is their way to go,
They'll risk damages, even fines.

Among the oil companies, the biggest and the "best."

The Exxon spill in Prince William Sound
Speaks for corporate pollution grand-scale,
For companies that lie by the pound,
For "risk projects" that may fail.
For promising "the damaged" refunds fair,
With no real intent to keep,
And secret payments to some who were "there."
While other folks are left to weep.

Birds of a feather, two cormorants, differing only in courage — the first a war hero, the second a war avoider.

> *Jim Wright was Speaker of the House,*
> *A war hero, credentials weighty;*
> *Served Texas in Congress since '55,*
> *Voted "most respected" in 1980.*
> *Resigned under fire in '89,*
> *Due to Ethics Committee charges,*
> *Including sales of* Reflections of a Public Man,
> *His book, which circumstance enlarges.*
> *He believed, in resigning, he'd paid his dues,*
> *As propitiation for all his wrongs;*
> *And district residents say they'd vote for him*
> *If he ran again — in throngs.*
> *Which makes one wonder if all those folks*
> *Feel other politicians aren't so bright;*
> *And Jim himself seems puzzled, 'cause*
> *The things he did were all so Wright.*
>
> *Senator Phil Gramm served for many years,*
> *He was a member of both Houses,*
> *Authored the Gramm/Rudman/Hollings Act,*
> *"Balance Federal Budget," he espouses.*
> *Yet no one did more than Senator Phil*
> *To postpone facing the national debt;*
> *He knew Congress sessions stand alone,*
> *Laws ignored to our country's regret.*
> *He played his cards for personal fame,*
> *And tricked the middle class;*
> *Played politics to gain jobs for his wife,*
> *Many times this came to pass.*
> *And, while Phil's known for avoiding war,*
> *Now takes a soldier's stance,*
> *Ready to fight, and face the gore,*
> *His target enemy, fire ants.*
> *He finds them worse than the VC,*
> *Dreams of them won't let him sleep,*

So he lobbies funds for their death decree,
A new job his wife could keep.

A prince of a fellow,

Charles H. Keating, Jr., was a big lawyer/financier,
A savings and loan swindler, stood the system on its ear;
He was sentenced to ten years in prison back in 1992,
For defrauding Lincoln Savings depositors, which is something he
did do.
He controlled the bank through holding company, American Conti-
nental,
And "the largest fraud" suit brought 'gainst him was hardly acci-
dental.
It cost taxpayers like you and me a king's ransom to make right,
For "the greediest man in America" had moved with great foresight,
In three plus years he looted the bank for 85,000 ounces of gold,
So his family could live in style unknown to kings of old.
He had a fleet of planes, far-flung homes, political influence that counts,
Contributed to five senators' campaigns, in varying amounts.
And they, in turn, intervened to have investigations slowed,
To find they were later criticized for paying the debt they owed.
Keating pushed junk bonds onto retirees through salesman that
would call,
Being told "the weak, the meek, and the ignorant are best targets of
all."
And figuring he might get the bank somehow out of hock,
By getting customers to buy worthless bonds he had in stock.
Implying that they were well backed by the FSLIC,
Which made the shares sound good to them, as they would to you
and me.
Keating now roams free, and it's known that he brags of his prison
time,
"I exercised there, added to my life," the man feels in his prime.

And the king of them all,

In the '80s Wall Street bore
Michael Milken to the fore.

A lad born on the Fourth of July,
And cheerleader at Birmingham High,
Who came to lead the brokerage crowd,
Lusting gold, with greed endowed,
Who got their customers to respond
To lures of each tempting yield junk bond.
These men, in suspenders, garish, bright,
Would sell their customers day and night,
Amassing for themselves such plunder,
That pirates of old would gasp in wonder
At these, who knew how best to skim
With nary a risk to life or limb.
And, when called upon to give account,
Most just walked off with full amount.
And, e'en those few who went to prison,
See Milken as a god who's risen!

Michael Milken was an honors man,
Graduate of Wharton School;
Came to Wall Street with a plan,
High-yield junk bonds were his tool.
And, when the jury indicted him,
On insider trading, conspiracy, fraud,
He plea bargained the government for a trim
To something far less broad.
He's done his time, and paid his fine
And, with 1.5 million ounces of gold,
American bank robbers, all in line,
Never made that much all told!
Milken now is free, and will say he
Doesn't consider his work a crime;
"I've never made a penny dishonestly,"
Says the cleverest of our time.

If attainder and corruption of blood are used, a thousand-name proscription list from a generation or two before your ascendancy should produce eight to twelve thousand descendants. A small number indeed, Mr. President. In your time, it would approximate only one person per thirty-five thousand citizens. A percentage allocation based on occupation might be appropriate for any selection process, since the actual number of those proscribed may be dictated by the severity of your problems.

Regardless of the total number, consider the following ratios: lawyer-politicians, 20 percent; politicians in general, 15 percent; regular lawyers, 15 percent; insurance company chief executive officers, 15 percent; stock and bond manipulators, 15 percent; larcenous savings and loan officials, 5 percent; environmental polluters, 5 percent; chief executive officers of companies in other fields, 5 percent. This would leave a reserve of 5 percent for judicial, pharmaceutical, media communication (television, newspaper, magazine, and radio), and a host of other professionals.

CHAPTER TWENTY-ONE

The Necessity of Conquest

❧

Conquest is more than just an exercise for gain; it is part of the ten-generation evolution of all great nations. That some nations fail at conquest while others succeed matters not. Mobilizing the country's armed forces and making war to acquire territory is the only way a country can climb out of its decadence and into a stable period of growth and prosperity. So it has been throughout history.

"War is one of the constants of history, and has not diminished with civilization or democracy," wrote Will and Ariel Durant in *The Lessons of History*. When Rome conquered the then-known world, the Pax Romana brought 210 years of world peace among the states within the Imperial frontiers, the longest period without war in the last 3,448 years of recorded history. (However, wars were fought during that period in countries untouched and unknown to Rome.) Tranquility was not Rome's purpose, only a by-product of profit by conquest.

Even newly installed leaders of small countries, which can never attain international consequence, attempt conquest and employ war to focus their countrymen on foreign bloodshed and away from domestic problems. This prevents the excesses of and grievances against the past regime from being resurrected and cast against the new order.

In my time, Cuba involved itself in a war in Angola and meddled in the affairs of various South American countries. These unsuccessful excursions by an insignificant country helped keep the Cuban leader in control of his country for more than a generation.

During the same period, the Shah of Iran hosted a world-class party and invited international notables. The party's theme was Persia. The stated goal was to establish that his Iran was as important to the world as Persia was in earlier times. Partygoers consumed one-third of the world's supply of 1961 vintage Lafite-Rothschild wine, but little else was accomplished. The reality of history escaped the Shah; he foolishly believed that money alone could recreate the past greatness of Persia. For many years, the support of the United States kept the Shah on the Peacock Throne. American endeavors were not enough, however. The Shah eventually lost control of the country because he tried to maintain his dictatorship without undertaking foreign conquest. He forfeited his country but managed to leave alive, albeit ailing. So perhaps the best one could say about the Shah is that he threw good parties.

The Shah's successor, the religious Khomeni, knew more about history than wine. He invited provocation, then attacked Iraq. Khomeni sacrificed hundreds of thousands of Iranians to keep intact his headship. Though he neither won nor lost his war, he kept his job. The living among his people revered him, and his hand-picked successor continued his cause.

Regardless of reasons offered or deduced, wars are instigated to protect or increase one individual's primacy. Without the catharsis of war, authoritative leaders are dislodged. Conquest can help maintain your leadership, Mr. President, while at the same time America becomes great again. In placing the nation on the course of conquest, only you will know when the time is right to capitalize on world political conditions. A decade one way or the other makes little difference.

Use the law of ten generations to track each mighty foreign power, friend or foe, because great nations move phase by phase through this seemingly inexorable pattern. Not all civilizations complete the cycle; some burst onto the scene with great vigor but vanish long before the tenth generation. China's Yüan (Mongol)

Dynasty demonstrates one such aborted attempt; it lasted only 108 years, 1260–1368. Nonetheless, when the ten-generation cycle itself is completed, it neither materially shortens nor lengthens, nor does the sequence of stages within it vary.

Identifying specific phases within ten-generation cycles is difficult and can be more easily accomplished through hindsight. Since each age within a cycle follows the well-worn groove of Outburst, Conquest, Commerce, Affluence, Intellect, and Decadence, in that exact sequence, it is more reliable to identify earlier completed ages and then deduce the nation's current phase. For instance, the Age of Conquest for the United States lasted eighty-seven years, 1846–1933. Japan's most recent Age of Conquest began in 1894; two generations later, in 1945, it ended with defeat at American hands.

At the end of the Conquest stage, countries destined for greatness unfailingly enter the season of Commerce, as did both America and Japan. Whether the Age of Conquest is prolonged by victory or shortened by defeat matters not. Circumstances shape the phases but not the cycle itself. Analysis of a decade of events assists in determining a particular phase; trying to make annual assessments yields little.

Interpret the following as you see fit. I see splendid advantages. At your ascendancy, the 1998 phase will be little changed. At the most, each country would be nearing or entering the subsequent phase in that country's cycle. Because of the wealth from their Age of Commerce and the undiminished resolve of their peoples, both Germany and Japan will have the potential to arm themselves as

[TABLE 7]

Current Nations' Tenth-Generation Phases

Country	Last Epoch	Current Ten Generation	1998 Phase
China	1644–1911	1912–ca. 2179	Conquest
Japan	1600–1867	1868–ca. 2135	Commerce
Germany	1686–1932	1933–ca. 2183	Commerce
Russia	1682–1916	1917–ca. 2151	Conquest
U.S.A.	1763–ca. 2012	ca. 2013–ca. 2263	Decadence

never before, not unlike the United States in 1940. Their strength should hold Russia in check. Japan, even with such capability, will be vulnerable to China's aspirations and its masses. Although years of adversarial relationships among their countries brought discord, a political triumvirate of Korea, Russia, and China, focused on conquering Japan, would force massive Japanese rearmament and defense spending. Japan, while not an avowed nuclear power, does have a nuclear arsenal already on hand at my time and should weather the storm using advanced technological weaponry coupled with the will of the Japanese people.

(The following I note only as trivia, since you need not concern yourself with such future events: Japan's next decadent ninth and tenth generations [2082-2135] will bring disaster to that nation. As China and others predominate, Japan will cease as a world power. Japan may still exist culturally, as do the now-stale countries of Greece, Italy, and Spain, or it may be assimilated wholly within China, as Etruria was by Rome.)

A N D now what of you, Mr. President? You could conquer the world — but why? Why would anyone want all of the circa 191 countries? Many are disease-ridden cesspools of humanity. Others, fractured by generations of ethnic or religious hatred, promise more pain than gain. You are not imbued with altruism, wanting to save these countries from their wretched conditions. Nor are you blinded by the lust for power, needing the entire world to bow down and acknowledge you. You know that if you attempted so much, for so little real gain, you would stand to lose everything. Even if you successfully conquered the world, America would be less secure than before that endeavor began: the penalty would be a full century of revolution.

Even when pursuing conquest, many more empires fail to rise again than succeed. Still, conquest is a matter of course in each ten-generation cycle of every successful civilization. War will come with America's Empire; best it be in conquest, not defense.

Keep in mind the words of Machiavelli: "Wars begin at the will of anyone, but they do not end at anyone's will." Consider carefully whom to conquer.

CHAPTER TWENTY-TWO

Selecting New Territories

❧

America's economic problems take time to cure. A vast number of Americans will fight to stay *in* a financial rut but not to get *out* of one. (Few realize that a rut is a grave with both ends open.) So while the economy is being revitalized, you will need a cause to engage the nation and rebuild America's greatness.

Some Americans are content to wait for an enemy to attack the United States; they say that defending their homes in this manner would, even at a great cost in American lives, unite the country. Others, of like mind, point out that although fewer American lives are lost when war is waged away from home, greater monetary costs occur. Heed not the fainthearted nor those concerned with hoarding their gold above saving American lives. In addition, there are stronghearted Americans who refuse to endorse unprovoked aggression; try to calm, not incite, them. Conquest at some point becomes a must for you, Mr. President, not an option.

Examine countries in the context of percentages of dominant versus nondominant citizens. Nations with the highest ratio of dominant citizens, although hardest to conquer, afterward become the most obedient and industrious. Countries populated mainly with nondominant people, while easier to overcome, thereafter prove the least productive and most unmanageable. Therefore, since the people will be troublesome, evaluate the worth of their land, minerals, and seas.

Totalitarianism, though differing in degrees of harshness, is a historic, natural way of life in countries where the dominant minority comprises less than 10 percent of the population. Over time, political labels change, but iron-handed rule does not. True democracy cannot exist when a population is overwhelmingly nondominant; neither can democracy flourish when exported to or implemented in such countries. China, where more than one in five humans live, had totalitarian rule during the thousands of years of its illustrious past. China's pseudo-democracy at my time is a sham; it is government by force, or no government at all.

In 1998, nations with the highest proportion of dominant mothers rearing dominant children and, in turn, the highest ratios of achievers are Japan, Germany, Israel, and, in a distant fourth, America. Even counting only non-Hispanic Caucasians, the United States still lags in the world lineup. American affluence has taken its toll; since 1946, dominant women have delivered and reared fewer children.

Prospering, thriving countries have higher percentages of dominant citizens than do unsuccessful countries. Worldwide medical advances limiting infant mortality altered the planet's allotment of high achievers versus low achievers. Nondominant populations multiplied mightily while, for nonmedical reasons, the dominant segments decreased. It is for these reasons, then, that the world's highest ratios of nondominant people reside in the Negro populations of Africa. Even the advent of *Slim* did little to slow the expanding numbers of low achievers there.

During the past century the increase of nondominant people was especially evident in Central and South American countries and in Mexico. Despite this, the proximity of these countries to our own and the value of their land, seas, and minerals are most advantageous. Certainly, you have already contemplated the benefits of bringing all the peoples of the American continents together. To add two North American, seven Central American, and thirteen South American countries under the United States flag presents a great undertaking, but this is a worthy goal: to bring security to America.

At each step of the way, have the willingness to back off from and temporarily stop further acquisitions. Deadline announcements will defeat you, as can unfilled promises of early conquest; it is better to give assurances that each conquest is the last, whether or not that is the case. Heed the admonition from Polybius twenty-one centuries ago: "Those who know how to win are much more numerous than those who know how to make proper use of their victories." Plan thoroughly for apt use of new territories.

Some nations on the American continents may wish to join forces with you. A guarantee of statehood with full American citizenship, including voting rights, could appeal to Argentina, Chile, Paraguay, Uruguay, and particularly Canada and Costa Rica, two nations with a large percentage of high achievers. Converts who fit the U.S. mold are more desirable than those brought to the fold by conquest. For the time being, forget statehood for Central and South American countries such as Brazil, El Salvador, Guatemala, and Nicaragua. Their populations are profoundly nondominant with few high achievers. Mandated control, although more costly, is preferable for governing these countries.

All twenty-four Caribbean island countries can be yours by bargaining or by conquest. Already American or not, select, or retain, only those that bring offshore security and future financial benefits to the United States. Avoid Haiti, the Dominican Republic, and Puerto Rico. Their populations equal one-half of all Caribbean countries, and the value of the three countries lumped together is less than that of Africa's least desirable country. These three countries will breed themselves out of existence. Enforce the Monroe Doctrine: block foreign influence to keep America secure.

Nothing unites a country more than a just war. Make your war just and righteous, Mr. President, otherwise it will parallel the war with Vietnam. Some Americans balked at fighting and fled the country; others complained of taxes to pay for a war begun without good cause. Americans of these stripes will be numerous at your time.

Mexico never forgot losing the 1846 war with the United States. Seven decades later, at 2:30 in the morning on March 9, 1916, Francisco "Pancho" Villa invaded the United States, attacking without warning the small town of Columbus, New Mexico. Villa told his three to four hundred soldier-bandits, "We're going to kill gringos, boys." Murder they did, shouting *Viva Villa! Viva Mexico! Muerte a los Americanos!* The town's doctor, the druggist, the grocery store owner, and two women were among a dozen unarmed citizens the Mexicans murdered. Colonel Slocum's American guards were drunk and deficient. Villa's sneak attack was successful. Two U.S. soldiers who managed to set up a machine gun and kill some Villistas were killed in turn, and the machine gun, ammunition, and other armaments disappeared. Buildings and homes were looted and herds of cattle were driven to Mexico. The Villistas left behind their dead and wounded. Colonel Slocum hanged five of the wounded.

Turn-of-the-century America was strong and resolute; it retaliated immediately. Americans of that era dealt in deeds, not debates. No time was wasted on hearings or building public support before taking action. Colonel Frank Tompkins mounted a calvary of thirty-two riders. That same day, he gave pursuit into Mexico, and by nightfall thirty Mexican soldiers were dead.

President Woodrow Wilson then ordered General John J. Pershing to lead a punitive expedition into Mexico to pursue Villa. Hundreds of Mexicans, innocent and otherwise, including a few Villistas, paid early debts to nature during eleven months of fighting, but Villa remained uncaptured. Mexicans loved the bandit Villa because he killed gringos, a manifestation of their loathing of the United States. Mexico made Villa, already a national hero, into a larger-than-life legend.

Mexico remembers well its defeat by the United States in 1846, when the government ceded nearly one-half of its realm. That conquest of Mexico ushered in America's first Age of Conquest. Further, the humiliation of America's punitive expedition of 1916 compounded Mexico's ongoing bitterness toward the United States. After that, time and again, Mexico's government retaliated against American financial interests in their country. One instance involved expropriating all American investment in and management of oil and gas companies in Mexico. It did not stop there.

For a century, good business in Mexico dictated *Tomar al gringo*. Beginning in 1964, Mexican nationals played a more deadly game in the United States: rob, rape, and murder the gringo, then run to safety in Mexico. Escalating in 1988, hundreds, then thousands, of Mexicans ventured into the United States, robbing, raping, and murdering American citizens. Mexican law forbade extradition of its citizens to the United States, and the United States stood by silently. American plunder bribed Mexican officials to let offenders live in peace as, again and again, they raided the United States and returned to Mexico. Truly, no other country presents you such an opportunity to create a "just" hatred and a "just" desire among Americans to avenge themselves.

By 1998, Mexicans, numbering tens of thousands, imitated Pancho Villa's cattle theft on a grander scale. Each week, convoys of stolen American automobiles entered Mexico, many presold to Mexicans before their theft. One make of truck became so popular that the American manufacturer increased production to meet the needs of Mexican thieves. Price was important, but pride was greater; the automobiles were stolen from gringos. Once, in a goodwill gesture, the Mexican government returned a few stolen vehicles to the American government, but nothing could resurrect Americans murdered by the modern Villistas. No Colonel Tompkins arose to retaliate. Federal bureaucrats did not even bother keeping separate records of Mexican crimes, as they did of terrorists from Iran, Iraq, and Syria.

Accepting these invasions without complaint, the acquiescent U.S. federal government downplayed the severity of criminal intrusions from Mexico by lumping their crimes with those committed by American-born Hispanics. Each crime, however atrocious, received primarily local and sometimes state attention but almost never warranted national notice as emanating from Mexico. America's weak federal government dreaded rankling the Mexican government, America's great trading partner — marijuana and cocaine for computers and hair dryers. Fear of offending Hispanic American voters silenced American politicians.

During this period, the best and the worst Mexicans came to the United States. The ambitious and high-achieving came to better themselves and, in turn, America. Additionally, first-rate laborers crossed the border illegally to work at jobs that welfare Americans no longer deigned to perform. But the villainous came solely to ravage. In Mexico, low-level crime is punished severely, torture being a standard tool of inquiry. Few of the poor own a car, much less a gun. After illegally entering the United States, numerous Mexicans buy a used car within months. For too many a pistol purchase soon follows.

A half-century ago, Mexico enjoyed a stable political climate. As with all countries having few achievers, Mexico, then and now, was ruled by a totalitarian government. It has a six-year presidency with power bordering on absolute. In 1945, under strong leadership, Mexico's peso currency equaled the strength of the U.S. dollar. The Mexican people were industrious, productive, and content. Mexico was a wealthy country by any standard. In that year, the Mexican government owned 8.4 million ounces of gold, more gold than was possessed by the Netherlands and an amount greater than that owned by the governments of Spain, Japan, Italy, Austria, and Germany combined. But by 1985, Mexico had squandered 72 percent of its gold. The governments of Spain, Japan, Italy, Austria, and Germany used those forty years to increase their gold holdings from 5.97 million gold ounces to 221.87 million gold ounces.

Weak Mexican leadership took its toll. Under profligate governments, Mexico steered its ship of state into an impenetrable and ever-expanding wall of low-achieving citizens. Prolific, nondominant Mexican breeders won out over anemic leadership. By 1998, corrupt Mexican leaders held sway in every field of endeavor. In 1998 the Federal District of Mexico, Mexico City, was reminiscent of 1761 Paris, France: half the nation's wealth was siphoned into the Federal District and half the poverty of Mexico suppurated there. Each six-year presidency came with a six-year license to steal — and grand thefts they were.

"A poor politician is indeed a poor politician." That particular Mexican politician spoke for all of his ilk. To serve the greed of a few, Mexicans were forced to pay monthly utility bills for water, electricity, and sewage *before* usage. Property taxes were demanded a year in advance. New and exotic taxes were assessed for almost everything under the sun, but the high and mighty managed to avoid paying them.

Each Mexican president set the stage for his hand-picked successor to fleece the country further. For instance, one president in

1976 authorized Mexican dollar-denominated bank accounts, called "Mex-dollars," to protect Mexicans against the vagaries of an unstable peso. The next president, in 1982, invalidated the dollar-denominated accounts and redeemed them, offering a choice — inflated pesos or near-worthless government bonds. In one day, politicians stole the equivalent of 37 million ounces of gold from honest Mexicans and reckless American depositors. Mexican politicians blithely called them "Ex-dollars." This world-class theft helped keep Mexico afloat for almost a decade.

Mexican lawmakers, after sharpening their bilking skills at home, plied their trade worldwide, emerging as world-class borrowers. In 1994, the North American Free Trade Agreement (NAFTA) created an unprecedented opportunity for greedy Mexican politicians and business leaders. Wary but foolish political leaders of a few industrialized countries loaned several million gold ounces to the Mexican government to do with as it saw fit. In addition to this, a smiling President William Clinton rushed to head the line, tendering 52 million ounces of gold. Elite U.S. banks pressured American politicians to make the loan, sharing in the spoils when some heretofore uncollectible Mexican loans were repaid. Large American banks became partners with Mexican swindlers at the expense of U.S. taxpayers.

The Mexican government's stated intentions to repay were admirable; their after-the-grants greed was less honorable. Over the following few months after NAFTA, government officials worked day and night to spend and steal. Politicians fought politicians to enrich themselves. They financially drained and bankrupted Mexico, but they still refused to call it quits. Before NAFTA, only one Mexican officially was known to have a net worth of over 2.5 million gold ounces. In less than a year the list expanded to ten more who had acquired a like net worth. Mexicans with a net worth of 2,500 gold ounces, including politicians and political appointees, became as plentiful as peanuts. Mexican politicians were pleased to gull Europe and Japan, but the satisfaction was small compared to getting even with the United States on a financial scale never before seen in Mexico.

These travesties will appear of little consequence to you, since Mexico's transgressions against the United States in your time are ten times worse in every category than they were at my time. Before your presidency, anarchy and open class warfare had erupted in Mexico and catapulted America into the crossfire of financial chaos and real bullets. Loaning gold to bankrupt, corrupt governments has many precedents, both in loans and in repayment failures. An enfeebled United States would send diplomats to negotiate peace between rebel leaders and the Mexican government along with new gold to replace old worthless Mexican loans. Though your predecessor may have received the Nobel Peace Prize for the former, both tenderings would fail.

Corrupt governments make poor stewards for land and sea management. In Mexico, huge reserves of oil and gas and of gold and silver are improperly tapped and mined, and millions of acres of fertile land lie fallow. The government sold fishing rights to Korea and other countries, rights that specifically limited the catch to certain species. Bribed officials looked the other way while all fish were taken.

Limited and intellectually inadequate schools keep the majority of the population mentally dull, while the education of the privileged class is second to none. Poor, illiterate Mexicans who steal from a railroad boxcar are severely punished; the "best and brightest" who steal the income from the government-owned railroad are rewarded with respect. The United States cannot fail to better manage Mexico's resources and improve the lot of non-elite Mexicans.

The millions of Mexicans who leave the country attest to the self-serving, corrupt ruling class. Those who escaped Ferdinand and Isabella's Spain, Louis XIV's France, Nazi Germany, Communist Russia, and Communist Cuba differ only in geography from those escaping Mexico and Central and South America: few citizens abandon countries that provide safe havens.

Mexicans who value gainful employment, honest government, and quality education but are denied all three will welcome you. Many hardworking Mexicans hunger for and would delight in the breakup of the millions of acres of government-owned *ejido* land. And there is no better way to reward American war veterans than with land grants in Mexico. Indeed, Mr. President, Mexico is a splendid new territory to add to the United States of America.

CHAPTER TWENTY-THREE

The Conquest of Mexico

❧

Replay America's first Age of Conquest. Invade Mexico. The United States took almost half of Mexico in 1846. Take the remainder.

At your time, Mexico will have some 150 million inhabitants, almost half the population of the United States. It would come to pass that many Mexican Americans would sever their cultural ties with Mexico when granted U.S. citizenship. They would choose to observe American holidays honoring an earlier America rather than celebrate Mexican national holidays in the United States. Shortly before the war with Mexico, I expect that a number of Mexican Americans will discard their Spanish surnames, choosing others of non-Spanish European origin; this will prove cohesive to your new America. In taking this action, they bear witness before all that they support your cause above all others.

Ensure that all American citizens of Mexican origin enjoy the full benefits of American citizenship during the war with Mexico. President Franklin Roosevelt, as commander in chief, exercised his war declaration authority to intern Japanese American citizens in guarded camps during World War II. Out of respect to those Mexican Americans who wholeheartedly chose America, do not establish similar internment camps for Mexican-American citizens. Rather, allow each to choose, in writing, either the United States or Mexico. Let those choosing Mexico go south in peace. But those who choose the United States but later consort with Mexico are wartime criminals of the vilest type. Let their pigmentation determine their destination — Africa or Siberia.

As has been the case with past wars, popular songs are the seeds of victory. The paucity of war paeans during the Vietnam War foretold defeat, as did the sad lament of ballads when Ireland last rebelled against the English. Reflecting the public mood, World War II lyrics invigorated a determined United States and whetted America's appetite for more victories in an already popular war. Use propaganda to build public support before and during the war with Mexico. This will bring about rousing martial music to further encourage citizens and troops alike.

After conquering Mexico, you will have to contend with no more than 5 percent of the population, or perhaps fewer, as many leaders will take their ill-gotten gains and flee the country. Before and during conquest, this same 5 percent will rail against you and stir the populace to fight your troops. Because the people of Mexico are brave, many Mexicans will listen to nationalistic exhortations and resist you.

Sway American and world opinion to your side, Mr. President. Use *mission*, a splendid and uplifting word — *mission* to free Mexico; *mission* to liberate Mexico; *mission* to civilize Mexico. Show Americans that the war to free Mexico brings jobs for Americans as well as international admiration. News such as this should have a tonic effect on the United States, as you need to reinforce in all the idea that America stands for something great, important, and successful.

Arrange matters so that Mexico appears the aggressor. Use propaganda to summon other civilized people to stand with the United States against Mexico — its illegal drug operations, its police state, its class warfare. Anticipate that, at first, world opinion will oppose you. Select the country that is most vociferous in denouncing the upcoming war with Mexico and vilify its government. Accuse that nation's leaders of secretly encouraging Mexico to fight. Assure the world that the price of that nation's support for Mexico is a piece of Mexico itself: Mexican leaders are offering Mexican territory as a bribe to that country for its public support.

In my time, citizens from all world countries, even those of our closest allies, voiced anti-American sentiments. America's downward spiral to your time increased the vituperations tenfold. Undoubtedly, some countries may attempt to capitalize on America's preoccupation with conquering Mexico. So during this period of international unrest, expect a revival of terrorism directed against Americans abroad. Keep an American military presence worldwide and treat foreign terrorism in the same previously successful manner, with one exception: do not commit ground troops. Retaliate with air and sea missiles and bombs. You do not need a second front.

Many governments will ignore the impending conquest, calling it an American problem. War in this hemisphere does not threaten interests in Asia and Europe to any great extent. (This is no different from times when the United States looked the other way during foreign slaughters.) These governments know, too, that you are strong enough to take them as well. If the conquest is completed quickly enough, most Asian and European countries may not be overly vocal in their protests. In addition, promise foreign nations that America will honor their Mexican investments and contractual agreements.

Ask Congress for a declaration of war against Mexico. Expect quick compliance. Should Congress delay, move forward under the shelter of your declaration of war against crime. Station troops, armor, planes, and missiles along the border with Mexico. Begin naval exercises in the Caribbean and Pacific. To increase the excitement, let hundreds of journalists and television news commentators accompany American troops into Mexico.

After the war to free Mexico begins, some European countries may condemn the United States as an aggressor nation and impose economic sanctions. Mobilize friendly American intellectuals to express their sense of outrage that those governments prefer a horde of Mexican murderers to the United States of America, the custodian of the European spirit.

In return for foreign support of American action, encourage the settling of old scores by those countries helpful during this period. Supply these friends of America with advanced weaponry. Let complacent, anti-American countries spend time defending their lives in what they believed was a safe, protected haven from which to criticize.

Since you already command the expertise, the strategy, and the tactics to complete the first conquest, that of Mexico, I have only a few suggestions. Consider again a casualty ratio of one American warrior for one hundred Mexican soldiers. Make this a real war, not the technological carnage it could be, thereby preserving the courage and honor of Mexico's armed forces and allowing America's military to take real pride in their victories. Anticipate armed support on behalf of Mexico from Central and South American volunteers, and even from other nations. Identify the heaviest concentration of foreign fighters and make these areas the fiercest battlegrounds. Here you change the ratios and exact severe punishment. Foreign volunteers will take home the message, some verbally, some physically.

Send a still-stronger message around the world. Should foreign involvement, such as arms shipments or military advisers, from outside the Americas occur (perhaps from China, Iran, Germany, Japan, Russia, or elsewhere), consider a demonstration of the might and resolve of the United States. Display what could be in store for any nation that ignores the Monroe Doctrine.

In America, after 1945, some believed a demonstration of the atom bomb in Tokyo's harbor would have brought peace without dispensing the nuclear death that occurred for residents of Hiroshima and Nagasaki. While doubtful, this is possible. Test that theory in Mexico. Assure Mexico that this action is not to be construed as part of the war, only as a demonstration for the benefit of foreign countries attempting to interfere.

Select a site surrounded by desert or mountains or both, such as the city of Durango, the adopted hometown of Pancho Villa. Give advance warning — the date and the time — of the forthcoming low-radiation neutron demonstration. Then erase that city forever. Durango and its larger-than-life bronze of Villa astride his horse will be reduced to dust and detritus. Only a few foolhardy souls will perish, and you will resolve the three-generations-old question of the merit of a nuclear display to prevent conflict before actual deployment. (As a goodwill gesture, Mr. President, and in good time, rebuild the highways around the city. The roads can circle the city's perimeter to avoid environmental dangers but still be close enough for future generations to view the rubble.)

In the event that a nuclear demonstration does not deter countries violating the Monroe Doctrine, select the strongest of the opportunist nations. Destroy that particular country's military presence in the Americas and devastate the home country. Again, beware of committing American troops to battle on foreign soil during the war with Mexico.

After the conquest of Mexico and before American troops march victoriously through the country, prepare the Mexican population for their entry. Provide the citizens of each city, town, and village with small American flags to welcome America's fighting men. Television will make much of the flag waving, especially by the children; a few countries may applaud, but most will not. Mr. President, please do not penalize your marching men for singing the song "Green Grow the Rushes."

Place the overall management of the country's affairs under an American viceroy, but assign the hands-on management of Mexico to the most stalwart of the country's middle-class and underprivileged idealistic defenders. Do not trust those Mexicans who sided with the United States; they are untrustworthy and, in time, will turn against you. For one year after the conquest, keep Mexico's Code Napoleon, with its provision of guilty until proven innocent, but establish American law in Mexico upon the conquest's first anniversary.

Rename the conquered territory and choose new names for the thirty-two states. Select a more convenient and healthier site for the Federal District, and build a new and less elaborate capitol. The old Federal District can become a splendid historical city.

History chronicles hundreds of short-lived conquests where the victor attempted direct rule without an accompanying edict for language change. Establish American English as the official tongue for this new territory, as did Hernan Cortes when he chose Spanish twenty generations earlier. While despising Cortes, Mexicans adore the language he forced on their Indian ancestors. Permit the personal use of Spanish, but require American English for all federal, state, municipal, and civil matters including the practice of education and business. Satellite communications can assist the new territory as it changes its education system to American English.

Mexican resentment will fester; radical changes and being under the United States' yoke make it inevitable. Make a permanent impression on all classes of Mexicans. Get their attention quickly with an easy-to-implement display of power that does not involve confiscation of property or citizen breath-departure. Suppress forever the civil rights of those with certain names; proscribe all Mexicans with these names, but limit the Decree of Attainder to Pains and Penalties. Without exception, bar all with these surnames from all future involvement in the territory, from voting or teaching, from holding elected or appointed government positions, from employment by the government or any company doing business with the government, and from practicing law. For example, abolish the following surnames, both patrilineal and matrilineal: Aguirre, Aranda, Barbosa, Baz, Bermudez, Bracho, Caballero, Cano, Carranza, Castro, Cisneros, Colomo, Covarrubias, Franco, Gallegos, Herrera, Luis, Mauricio, Montoya, Nava, Pasero, Quiñones, Sanfelize, Vargas, and de Vega.

Some individuals with these surnames achieved success by deceit. Even though these cognomens are not overly abundant in Mexico, their inclusion should bring about the intended results. (Another list of twenty-five prosperous family names, equally skimpy in sheer numbers of Mexicans, would suffice.) Hold in abeyance the more widespread surnames of Garcia, Gonzalez, and Sanchez for a second pains and penalties blacklist. Use an additional surname only if the outcome of bringing swift compliance from a conquered people proves unsatisfactory. To avoid confusion, do not permit American citizens with a taboo surname to enter the new territory or conduct business there.

People have a lifetime love affair with their names. That you simply ban certain surnames in a matter of minutes will not be lost upon the millions of Mexicans who have different names. Some of those listed will attempt to change the names of their children, and a few will try to change their own names. Let them change the names of their offspring, as this is of little consequence. Your power is acknowledged. Even without decree, few Germans of my time are named Adolf Hitler, and no Mexican female is named Malinche.

Enjoy your successful conquest! But remember that lesser leaders at this point savor victory and procrastinate. Other leaders, overconfident in victory, foolishly rush the goal of future conquest too quickly. Do neither.

CHAPTER TWENTY-FOUR

The New American Hemisphere

The Age of Decadence in the United States produced the largest drug addiction in history. In 1998, the per-person consumption of marijuana, cocaine, heroin, and their derivatives, along with chemically compounded illegal stimulants, was eight times that of China at the peak of its two hundred years of addiction. And when you became president, illegal drug usage in America was ten times worse than in my time.

The natural law of supply and demand is difficult to repeal through government intervention against supply. Although supply and demand balance ultimately, it is demand that controls supply. The United States did nothing to eliminate demand, foolishly thinking it adequate to attempt to arrest the supply side of the equation. So, since you eradicated illegal drug demand in America, no action is needed to purge supply. By nature, it goes away. Still, a splendid, virtuous, and righteous propaganda opportunity awaits you. Capitalize on the past drug problems in America.

Mexico, a sizable producer and supplier for our country's drug addiction, was also the world's largest funnel for smuggling illegal drugs of other countries into the United States. Mexico was rife with drug lords who profited mightily from America's malaise. Illegal drug profiteering provided funds for bribing Mexican officials to secure protection from Mexican law.

Mexican drug dealers held the Shangfang sword and used it ruthlessly; at their direction, thousands of illegal drug competitors, from all social strata, fell victim to that sword. American tourists were also fair game, most often slaughtered for trivial reasons. An American drug enforcement agent was slowly tortured to death while Mexican law officers and top government officials looked on. A drug chieftain massacred a Roman Catholic cardinal and his entourage. High-level Mexican officials who were unfriendly to drug cartels were murdered. Illegal drug profits, invested in kidnapping foreigners and prominent Mexican businessmen and family members for ransom, provided high returns to Mexico's organized crime families.

Consider busying the new territory's people in seeking out these thousands of past drug masters, their employees, and the officials they bribed. Offer copious rewards; then, with profuse appreciation and public fanfare, tender the rewards. After thorough investigations, the viceroy's hand-picked Mexican judges can deal with the deluge of those who prospered servicing America's past drug addiction. Be fair. Those bearing false witness — whether to reap rewards, seek revenge, or for whatever reason — should be convicted and punished as if they had committed the offense charged against the wrongfully accused.

Although lists of wrongdoers, drug dealers or otherwise, were not accepted in the United States, permit this in the new territory. Let Mexicans right past wrongs; grant a one-year grace period for them to purge the country of criminals. This includes removing however many lower-, middle-, and upper-class Mexican criminals they deem proper. As Mexicans are getting even for generations of criminal wrongdoing, accept their lawful decisions without question. Allow the Mexican judicial system to exact retribution. Mr. President, let the world know that, for a year, the United States has washed its hands of indicting, trying, and punishing Mexican wrongdoers.

Make these show trials without peer. Public fascination with television, particularly those programs depicting courtroom drama, will guarantee record world audiences. Television offerings in any country, no matter how lurid, cannot compete with true-life portrayals of righteous revenge. Worldwide, viewers will be riveted twenty-four hours a day, seven days a week, as Mexican justice is dispensed by Mexican judges. Even though drug dealers and their accomplices were the designated targets of denunciation, the courtroom drama will detail, for the first time, the depth of upper-class Mexican crime and corruption. These disclosures will hold center stage, although ordinary criminals will provide comic relief. Have your viceroy require that court proceedings be conducted solely in Spanish, not American English. This singular deviation in language use serves your most important agenda — the continuation of conquest — by guaranteeing large television audiences in Spanish-speaking Central and South American countries.

For many years, even before my time, Mexican law did not permit the death penalty for any crime, regardless of its severity, except by military courts, who dared not use that authority. This benefited primarily the elite. Their crimes loomed so large and heinous that they feared another Mexican revolution and predictable death penalties most of all. Mexican history made real to them earlier revolutionary wrath that cost their less-than-illustrious ancestors their lives.

The law against the death penalty need not survive your conquest, but the anger of the wronged will. New freedoms enjoyed the most by liberated people are those denied the longest; they receive the freest rein. The fear that Mexican citizens have of the privileged class crystallized long ago into hate, so expect few incarcerations since, historically, Mexicans seem predisposed to firing squads.

With much ado and international publicity, initiate a white bean drawing for those who were given the penalty of maximum punishment. Since so many will be sentenced daily, prepare lots of one thousand beans — nine hundred black, one hundred white. Let God decide who expires and who respires. And let pigmentation determine the destination for those who draw the white bean, the saved — Africa or Siberia. (Naturally, the new territory bears the overseas maintenance costs of those rescued.) At small cost, you benefit by keeping these few in the land of the living. Mexicans wonder at your generosity and remember the black bean drawing they used on the American Mier Expedition.

Central and South American countries will erupt in class warfare as the show trials run their course. When efforts to prevent television viewing in these countries fail, the nations will split into factions. Some will strive to survive, some will straddle, and others will fight for purposeless control. A few will cry out to the United States to intervene and bring order to replace chaos and anarchy. Central and South American governments, attempting to unite the people against America, will be powerless against uprisings by the vengeful who wait no longer for retribution. Besides common looters, intriguers who smell opportunity will add to the mayhem.

As leaders of those nations fly away with the numbers of their secret foreign accounts and what loot they can carry, countries south of Mexico that have not already been offered and accepted American statehood resemble dominoes set on end. Mexico's surrender and ensuing show trials trigger the fall. As their generals switch sides willy-nilly, confusion reigns until their soldiers join the looters. Then, anarchy.

And let anarchy prevail. The value of these countries lies not in the people but in the land, minerals, and sea. As with all power struggles, two factions finally emerge in each country and war for sole control. Since former borders become meaningless, both sides ally with forces from nearby countries and occupy themselves with posturing, negotiating, and appeasing. Between interludes of truce, they kill each other.

Any country that accepted American statehood will be unaffected internally by the chaos surrounding it. They require only American armor to hold their borders safe against unwanted refugees. Mexico, after the conquest, will need the same protection against refugees fleeing from other countries. Refugees, particularly early ones, who genuinely want to join the United States and fight their countrymen are a special issue. Even though it contradicts sound military judgment, perhaps compassion will permit you to find a way to utilize their services.

S E T no timetable for completing conquest. Bide your time, Mr. President. Haste is unnecessary. Concern yourself only with intervention from outside the Americas. Nature abhors a vacuum, and a vacuum of consequence will emerge as firestorms rage in Central and South America. The bulk of your military, held in abeyance for such contingency, along with fighters fresh from one conquest and not mired down on multiple fronts, can either face down or lethally put down foreign intrusions.

In time, countries in Central and South America reach that low point when the people lose their appetite for revenge against each other or for a fight with the United States. They hope only to survive. When the Four Horsemen of the Apocalypse appear and one faction is poised to annihilate the other, bring this territory into the American fold. Ally yourself with the weaker side and attack the stronger.

Add only one new territory at a time, as the largest threat remains from nations outside the Americas. The order in which you add territories matters not a whit; just save for last those countries that rebuffed your offer of statehood. Grant their people additional time to punish the leaders who led them astray, little different from the Carthaginians punishing their leaders over two millennia before.

After each conquest, permit only one month for the wronged to wreak retribution. If they tarry not, this time is ample to settle generations-old disputes. Refrain from intervening, except for judicious personal pardons to endear yourself to a chosen few. This ambiguity will go unnoticed, as sufficient Central and South American wrongdoers abound to satisfy even the most vengeful of the wronged. Show trials, as conducted in Mexico, are no longer necessary; neither is worldwide propaganda or publicity. Only the local inhabitants need to see the power of the United States. After a month, establish American law and order.

Canada, by this time, assuredly will have petitioned and become an honored state of America. Quebec? I have no idea. Perhaps leave Quebec alone as the only foreign nation in the Americas. The Vatican does not disrupt Italy; neither would Quebec disturb the United States. Quebec could be a quaint throwback to an earlier time and a testament to American benevolence.

A few Central and South American countries may suffer greater percentages of casualties than did Germany and Japan during World War II, but their postwar reactions will differ greatly. Germany and Japan, populated with large percentages of dominant people, were just as obedient in defeat as they were in war. Their needs to accomplish were channeled into rebuilding ruins, constructing new factories, and producing, in one generation, world industrial leaders. History recognizes no such achievements from primarily nondominant countries either before or after conquest.

Following the formalities of surrender and the grace period to avenge old wrongs, hostilities will continue in Mexico and those countries further south. Although expected, this is still a thorny aspect of conquering countries with predominately nondominant populations. While the majority of the inhabitants want to rebuild their lives, dissidents still desire to destroy. Many criminals, misfits, and malcontents will flee both American soldiers and the wrath of their own countrymen to find refuge and establish bases in the mountains and sparsely inhabited rural areas. They apply the tools of their trade, kidnapping and murder, to gain recognition and glory, as they style themselves freedom fighters and hope to become folk heros. Permit none of this.

North, Central, and South America are now yours. You can afford to be magnanimous. Your sense of personal accomplishment and your visualizations of wonderful changes for the people of the new territories make you susceptible to calls for amnesty, diplomacy, negotiation, or even to wooing the remaining misfits and malcontents to your side. Keep the raw nerve of fallibility exposed. Harden your heart and deal ruthlessly with the local bandits and those who join them, but do so privately. Publicity served you well in executing American policy during and after the war with Mexico; however, you no longer need to serve notice of the might of the United States. Privacy denies these groups the fame they angle for with martyrdom.

Without foreign support and supplies, native ingenuity cannot prevail. At an earlier time, the United States permitted the army and armor of China to supply and fight alongside North Koreans during the Korean Conflict. Outright permissiveness allowed Russia and China to supply North Vietnam to the detriment of America. The duration of your armed conflict is tied directly to the enforcement of the Monroe Doctrine.

These circumstances offer a splendid occasion for your child-development school charges to gain battlefield experience, if their maturation matches your conquest timetable. Your student military can implement your policies against homegrown bandits and their support groups. No amnesty, no quarter, only extermination. Even without publicity, word of their successes would spread among their peers and the schools' students. Further, the swiftness of their victories will gain high regard from the people in the new territories. This respect will serve your graduates well in the future when they govern these same provinces.

T o t a l victory produces a shield of invincibility. Now free from all restraints of society, you can have your way in any endeavor you choose and with any person in any manner. This day, the greatest day of your life, is also the most perilous. I again caution you against conquering the rest of the world. Perhaps this is my most meaningful counsel. Let some future fool bring about Armageddon. Ask God to help you bank your fires of ambition and lead you in rebuilding America. Ask Him to show you the way to enjoy the love and devotion of this great nation's people for America's Man on Horseback.

Whatever else I could offer you now would be mundane. You prevented a second American Civil War, saving thousands, perhaps millions, of American lives. Further, you provided future security for the Empire of the United States and set the stage for America to enter the most splendid Age of Commerce the world has ever seen, while at the same time presenting magnificent opportunities for all people in the Americas. In time, each territory will achieve statehood. At some future date, a president of the United States will come from what was once a territory. He will praise you, in American English, as the Father of the American Empire.

Mr. President, I close believing that I have helped you. God be with you.

No Better Friend • No Worse Enemy

So stated the epitaph on Sulla's monument in the Campus Martius. Sulla wanted all to know that he never neglected to repay the kindness of a friend or the hurt of an enemy.

There are those who spend a lifetime taking and rarely giving; they are the most numerous. There are those who give and receive in equal amounts; though numbering few, they are to be congratulated. There are those who gave more than they received; I speak for them.

Should you believe that my counsel truly benefited you, Mr. President, then I humbly make my request. Please accept a private list of names, small in number, to add to the lists that you receive.

Thank you,
Guy Roy Odom

Bibliography

Adams, Brooks. 1896. *The Law of Civilization and Decay: An Essay on History.* 2nd ed. Vintage Books, 1955.

Adams, James Truslow, ed.-in-chf. 1951. *Dictionary of American History, vol. 1.* 2nd rev. ed. Charles Scribner's.

Adamson, Robert. 1908. *The Development of Greek Philosophy.* Blackwood & Sons.

Allport, Gordon W., and Henry S. Odbert. 1936. *Trait-Names: A Psycho-lexical Study.* Psychological Review.

Andreasen, Nancy C. 1984. *The Broken Brain: The Biological Revolution in Psychiatry.* Harper & Row.

Antonov-Ovseyenko, Anton. 1981. *The Time of Stalin: Portrait of a Tyranny.* Trans. George Saunders. Harper & Row.

Appleton, R. B. 1922. *Greek Philosophy.* Methuen & Co.

Aretz, Gertrude. 1927. *Napoleon and His Women Friends.* Lippincott.

Armstrong, A. H. 1959. *An Introduction to Ancient Philosophy.* New Press.

Arnold, Magda B. 1960. *Emotion and Personality.* 2 vols. Columbia UP.

Asimov, Isaac. 1982. *Asimov's Biographical Encyclopedia of Science and Technology.* 2nd rev. ed. Doubleday.

———. 1985. *Isaac Asimov On the Human Body and the Human Brain.* Bonanza Books.

Atrill, Verne. 1981. *The Freedom Manifesto.* Dimensionless Science.

Ausubel, David P., and Edmund V. Sullivan. 1970. *Theory and Problems of Child Development.* 2nd ed. Grune & Stratton.

Bachofen, J. J. 1926. *Myth, Religion, and Mother Right.* Trans. Ralph Manheim. Princeton UP, 1967.

Baker, Timothy. 1966. *The Normans.* Macmillan.

Banking and Monetary Statistics 1941–1970. 1976. Bd. of Govs., Fed. Reserve.

Barber, Noel. 1973. *The Sultans*. Simon & Schuster.

Barlow, Frank. 1965. *William I and the Norman Conquest*. English UP.

Bateson and Jaeckel. 1974. Imprinting: Correlations Between Activities of Chicks During Training and Testing. *Animal Behaviour*. 22.

Benn, Alfred W. 1914. *The Greek Philosophers*. Smith, Elder.

Bettelheim, Bruno. 1969. *The Children of the Dream: Communal Child-Rearing and American Education*. Avon Books.

Binswanger, Harry, ed. 1986. *The Ayn Rand Lexicon: Objectivism from A to Z*. New American Library.

Blackstone, Sir William. n.d. *Commentaries on the Laws of England, vol. 1*. Ed. William Carey Jones. Bancroft-Whitney, 1915.

Bock, Alan W. 1995. *Ambush at Ruby Ridge: How Government Agents Set Randy Weaver Up and Took His Family Down*. Dickens Press.

Bois, J. Samuel. 1966. *The Art of Awareness: A Textbook on General Semantics and Epistemics*. 3rd ed. Wm. C. Brown, 1979.

Boorstin, Daniel J. 1987. *Hidden History*. Harper & Row.

Bowers, Claude G. 1925. *Jefferson and Hamilton*. Houghton Mifflin.

Braddy, Haldeen. 1955. *Cock of the Walk: The Legend of Pancho Villa*. U of New Mexico P.

Bramblett, Claud A. 1976. *Patterns of Primate Behavior*. Mayfield Publishing.

Branden, Nathaniel. 1969. *The Psychology of Self-Esteem: A New Concept of Man's Psychological Nature*. Nash Publishing.

Briffault, Robert. 1927. *The Mothers*. Abr. ed. Ruskin House, 1959.

Brough, James. 1977. *The Ford Dynasty: An American Story*. Doubleday.

Brown, Archie, John Fennell, Michael Kaser, and H. T. Willetts, gen. eds. 1982. *The Cambridge Encyclopedia of Russia and the Soviet Union*. Cambridge UP.

Brown, Robert. 1975. Following and Visual Imprinting in Ducklings Across a Wide Age Range. *Developmental Psychobiology*. Jan.

Brumbaugh, Robert S. 1964. *The Philosophers of Greece*. Thomas W. Crowell.

Bryson, Bill. 1990. *The Mother Tongue: English and How It Got that Way*. William Morrow.

———. 1994. *Made in America: An Informal History of the English Language in the United States*. Avon Books.

Burke, Charles. 1975. *Aggression in Man*. Lyle Stuart.

Burns, James MacGregor. 1978. *Leadership*. Harper & Row.

Bury, J. B., and Russell Meiggs. 1900. *A History of Greece to the Death of Alexander the Great*. 4th rev. ed. St. Martin's, 1978.

Canning, John. 1967. *100 Great Kings, Queens and Rulers of the World*. Taplinger.

Carmichael, Joel. 1976. *Stalin's Masterpiece: The Show Trials and Purges of the Thirties — The Consolidation of the Bolshevik Dictatorship.* St. Martin's.

Caro, Robert A. 1974. *The Power Broker: Robert Moses and the Fall of New York.* Vintage Books.

———. 1982. *The Years of Lyndon Johnson: The Path to Power.* Alfred A. Knopf.

———. 1990. *The Years of Lyndon Johnson: Means of Ascent.* Alfred A. Knopf.

Chapin, Bradley. 1964. *The American Law of Treason: Revolutionary and Early National Origins.* U of Washington P.

Christian, Shirley. 1985. *Nicaragua: Revolution in the Family.* Random House.

Collier, Peter, and David Horowitz. 1976. *The Rockefellers: An American Dynasty.* Holt, Rinehart.

Connolly, Cyril (Palinurus). 1945. *The Unquiet Grave.* Viking Press.

Cooke, Jacob E. 1967. *Alexander Hamilton: A Profile.* Hill & Wang.

Cookson, Peter W., Jr., and Caroline Hodges Persell. 1985. *Preparing for Power: America's Elite Boarding Schools.* Basic Books.

Corvo, Frederick B. 1931. *A History of the Borgias.* Modern Library.

Council on Environmental Quality and U.S. Dept. of State. 1980. *The Global 2000 Report to the President: Entering the Twenty- First Century,* vol. 1. USGPO.

———. 1981. *Global Future: Time to Act. Report to the President on Global Resources, Environment and Population.* USGPO.

Creasy, Sir Edward S. 1878. *History of the Ottoman Turks.* Bentley.

Crow, John A. 1965. *Italy: A Journey Through Time.* Harper & Row.

Darwin, Charles. 1859 and 1871. *The Origin of Species and The Descent of Man.* Modern Library, n.d.

Davidson, James Dale, and William Rees-Mogg. 1987. *Blood in the Streets: Investment Profits in a World Gone Mad.* Summit Books.

Davies, Reginald T. 1984. *The Golden Century of Spain: 1501–1521.* AMS Press.

Descola, Jean. 1970. *The Conquistadors.* Trans. Malcolm Barnes. Augustus M. Kelley.

Diederich, Bernard. 1981. *Somoza and the Legacy of U.S. Involvement in Central America.* E. P. Dutton.

Dimont, Max I. 1971. *The Indestructible Jews: An Action-Packed Journey Through 4,000 Years of History.* New America Library.

Diner, Helen. 1965. *Mothers and Amazons: The First Feminine History of Culture.* Trans. and Ed. John P. Lundin. Julian Press.

Dobson, James. 1970. *Dare to Discipline.* Bantam Books.

Doukas. 1975. *Decline and Fall of Byzantium to the Ottoman Turks.* Wayne State UP.

Drake, Henry L. 1958. *The People's Plato.* Philosophical Library.

Durant, Will. 1933. *The Story of Philosophy.* Simon & Schuster.

Durant, Will and Ariel. 1935–1975. *The Story of Civilization.* 11 vols. Simon & Schuster.

———. 1968. *The Lessons of History.* Simon & Schuster.

Effect of Mother on the Development of Aggressive Behavior in Rats. 1975. *Developmental Psychobiology.* Jan.

Eiserer and Hoffman. 1974. Acquisition of Behavioral Control by the Auditory Features of an Imprinting Object. *Animal Learning and Behaviour.* Nov.

———. 1974. Imprinting of Ducklings to a Second Stimulus When a Previously Imprinted Stimulus is Occasionally Presented. *Animal Learning and Behaviour.* May.

The Emergence of Man. 19 vols. 1972–1975. Time-Life.

The New Encyclopaedia Britannica. 1985. 32 vols. Encyclopaedia Britannica.

Encyclopaedia Judaica, 1971. vol. 13. Macmillan.

Encyclopaedia Judaica Decennial Book: 1973–1982. 1982. Keter Publishing House.

The Europa Year Book 1985: A World Survey. 2 vols. 1985. Europa Publications.

Eysenck, H. J., and Leon Kamin. 1981. *The Intelligence Controversy.* John Wiley.

Faber, Doris. 1968 and 1978. *The Presidents' Mothers.* St. Martin's.

Fairbanks, Arthur. 1898. *The First Philosophers of Greece.* Kegan, Paul, Trench, Tribner.

Fancher, Raymond E. 1985. *The Intelligence Men: Makers of the IQ Controversy.* W. W. Norton.

Fast, Howard. 1968. *The Jews: Story of a People.* Dell, 1982.

Fehrenbach, T. R. 1973. *Fire and Blood: A History of Mexico.* Bonanza Books, 1985.

Felsenthal, Carol. 1981. *The Sweetheart of the Silent Majority: The Biography of Phyllis Schlafly.* Doubleday.

Field, G. C. 1930. *Plato and His Contemporaries.* Methuen & Co.

Fite, Warner. 1934. *The Platonic Legend.* Charles Scribner's.

Flexner, James T. 1978. *The Young Hamilton: A Biography.* Little, Brown.

Fosdick, Harry Emerson. 1938. *A Guide to Understanding the Bible: The Development of Ideas Within the Old and New Testaments.* 8th ed. Harper & Row.

Foy, Felician A., ed. 1984. *Catholic Almanac 1985.* Our Sunday Visitor.

Friday, Nancy. 1977. *My Mother/My Self: The Daughter's Search for Identity.* Delacorte Press.

Galdi, Theodor W., Caleb Rossiter, and Alfred Reifman. 1982. *Costs and Benefits of U. S. Foreign Aid.* Library of Congress. Oct. 25.

Galton, Sir Francis. 1892. *Hereditary Genius: An Inquiry into Its Laws and Consequences.* 2nd ed. Meridian Books, 1962.

Garrison, Robert J., V. Elving Anderson, and Sheldon C. Reed. 1968. Assortative Marriage. *Eugen. Quart.* 15:2.

Gibbon, Edward. 1776–1788. *The Decline and Fall of the Roman Empire.* 2 vols. Encyclopaedia Britannica, 1978.

Gibbons, Herbert A. 1968. *The Foundation of the Ottoman Empire.* Frank Cass.

Glubb, John B. 1969. *A Short History of the Arab Peoples.* Dorset Press, 1988.

———. 1973. *Soldiers of Fortune: The Story of the Mamlukes.* Dorset Press.

———. 1976. *The Fate of Empires and Search for Survival.* William Blackwood, 1981.

Goertzel, Victor and Mildred. 1962. *Cradles of Eminence.* Little, Brown.

Goodall, Jane. 1971. *In the Shadow of Man.* Houghton Mifflin.

———. 1986. *The Chimpanzees of Gombe: Patterns of Behavior.* Belknap Press.

Gould, Stephen Jay. 1981. *The Mismeasure of Man.* W. W. Norton.

Grant, Michael. 1987. *The Rise of the Greeks.* Charles Scribner's.

Grun, Bernard. 1975. *The Timetables of History: A Horizontal Linkage of People and Events.* Simon & Schuster, 1982.

Grunberger, Richard. 1971. *The 12-Year Reich.* Holt, Rinehart.

Haffner, Sebastian. 1941. *Germany: Jekyll and Hyde.* E. P. Dutton.

Hall, Kermit L., ed.-in-chf. 1992. *The Oxford Companion to the Supreme Court of the United States.* Oxford UP.

Hamburg, David A., and Elizabeth R. McCowen, eds. 1979. *Perspectives on Human Evolution,* Vol. V: *The Great Apes.* Benjamin/Cummings.

Hamilton, Allan M. 1910. *The Intimate Life of Alexander Hamilton.* Duckworth.

Hardie, W. F. R. 1936. *A Study in Plato.* Clarendon Press.

Harper's Bible Dictionary. 1961 ed.

Hayakawa, S. I. 1939. *Language in Thought and Action.* 3rd ed. Harcourt Brace, 1972.

Herold, J. Christopher, ed. and trans. 1955. *The Mind of Napoleon: A Selection From his Written and Spoken Words.* Columbia UP, 1961.

Hinde, R. A. 1966. *Animal Behaviour.* McGraw-Hill.

Hitler's Secret Conversations: 1941–1944. 1953. Farrar, Straus.

Hitler's Words. 1944. American Council on Public Affairs.

Hitti, Philip K. 1961. *The Near East in History.* Van Nostrand.

———. 1966. *A Short History of the Near East.* Van Nostrand.

The Holy Bible: Old and New Testaments in the King James Version. Ref. ed. Thomas Nelson, 1976.

Howe, Irving. 1976. *World of Our Fathers: The Journey of the East European Jews to America and the Life They Found and Made.* Harcourt Brace.

Ibn Khaldun. n.d. *The Muqaddimah: An Introduction to History.* Trans. Franz Rosenthal. Abr. and Ed. N. J. Dawood. Princeton UP, 1967.

Inalcik, Halil. 1973. *The Ottoman Empire.* Weidenfeld & Nicolson.

International Financial Statistics. 1985. IMF. Nov.

The Interpreter's Dictionary of the Bible: An Illustrated Encyclopedia. 4 vols. Abingdon Press, 1962.

Irvine, William. 1955. *Apes, Angels, and Victorians: The Story of Darwin, Huxley, and Evolution.* Time-Life.

Jacob, Francois. n.d. *The Logic of Life: A History of Heredity.* Trans. Betty E. Spillmann. Pantheon Books, 1973.

Jacquard, Albert. 1984. *In Praise of Difference: Genetics and Human Affairs.* Trans. Margaret M. Moriarty. Columbia UP.

———. 1985. *Endangered by Science?* Trans. Margaret M. Moriarty. Columbia UP.

Jay, Antony. 1968. *Management and Machiavelli: An Inquiry into the Politics of Corporate Life.* Holt, Rinehart.

Jennings, Eugene E. 1960. *An Anatomy of Leadership: Princes, Heroes, and Supermen.* McGraw-Hill, 1972.

Jensen, Arthur R. 1980. *Bias in Mental Testing.* Free Press.

———. 1981. *Straight Talk About Mental Tests.* Free Press.

The Jerome Biblical Commentary, Vol. I. 1968. Prentice-Hall.

John, Eric, ed. 1964. *The Popes: A Concise Biographical History.* Hawthorn Books.

Jones, Landon Y. 1980. *Great Expectations: America and the Baby Boom Generation.* Coward, McCann, & Geoghegan.

Kamin, Leon J. 1974. *The Science and Politics of I.Q.* Lawrence Erlbaum.

Karlsson, Jon L. 1978. *Inheritance of Creative Intelligence.* Nelson-Hall.

Katznelson, Ira. 1976. *Black Men, White Cities: Race, Politics, and Migration in the United States, 1900–1930, and Britain, 1948–68.* U of Chicago P.

Kaufmann, Yehezkel. 1937–1956. *The Religion of Israel: From Its Beginnings to the Babylonian Exile.* Trans. and Abr. Moshe Greenberg. U of Chicago P, 1960.

Kearns, Doris. 1976. *Lyndon Johnson and the American Dream.* Harper & Row.

Kennedy, Paul. 1987. *The Rise and Fall of the Great Powers: Economic Change and Military Conflict from 1500 to 2000.* Random House.

Kirk, G. S. 1959. *Heraclitus: The Cosmic Fragments.* Cambridge UP.

Klauder, Francis J. 1971. *Aspects of the Thought of Teilhard de Chardin.* Christopher Gordon.

Kortepeter, Carl M. 1972. *Ottoman Imperialism During the Reformation: Europe and the Caucasus.* New York UP.

Kuhn, Thomas S. 1962. *The Structure of Scientific Revolutions.* 2nd ed., enl. U of Chicago P, 1970.

Langer, Walter C. 1972. *The Mind of Adolf Hitler.* Basic Books.

Leakey, Richard E. 1981. *The Making of Mankind.* E. P. Dutton.

Leakey, Richard E., and Roger Lewin. 1977. *Origins: What New Discoveries Reveal About the Emergence of our Species and its Possible Future.* E. P. Dutton.

Leopold, Aldo. 1966. *A Sand County Almanac.* Ballantine Books.

Lerner, Alan C. 1982. Why Supply-Side Economics Is Not Working: A Wall Street Perspective. Address to Conf. Spons. Federal Reserve Bank of Atlanta and Emory University Law and Economics Center. March.

Lewontin, R. C., Steven Rose, and Leon J. Kamin. 1984. *Not In Our Genes: Biology, Ideology, and Human Nature.* Pantheon Books.

Library of Nations. 20 vols. 1985–1988. Time-Life.

Lieberman, Jethro K. 1992. *The Evolving Constitution: How the Supreme Court Has Ruled on Issues from Abortion to Zoning.* Random House.

Limbaugh, Rush. 1992. *The Way Things Ought to Be.* Pocket Books.

Lingeman, Richard. 1980. *Small Town America: A Narrative History 1620–The Present.* G. P. Putnam's.

Lorenz, Konrad. 1966. *On Aggression.* Trans. Marjorie Kerr Wilson. Bantam Books.

———. 1971. *Studies in Animal and Human Behaviour,* Vol. II. Harvard UP.

McClellan, Grant, ed. 1981. Immigrants, Refugees, and U.S. Policy. *The Reference Shelf.* 52:6. H. W. Wilson.

McClelland, David C. 1961. *The Achieving Society.* Free Press.

———. 1975. *Power: The Inner Experience.* Irvington.

———. 1985. *Human Motivation.* Scott.

MacEwan, Arthur. 1990. *Debt and Disorder: International Economic Instability and U.S. Imperial Decline.* Monthly Review.

Mackay, Harvey B. 1988. *Swim with the Sharks Without Being Eaten Alive.* William Morrow.

McKeon, Richard, ed. 1941. *The Basic Works of Aristotle.* Random House.

McNeill, William H. 1976. *Plagues and Peoples.* Doubleday.

Machiavelli, Niccolo. n.d. *The Discourses.* Trans. Leslie J. Walker. Ed. Bernard Crick. Penguin Books, 1974.

———. *The Prince.* n.d. Trans. George Bull. Penguin Books, 1981.

———. *Florentine Histories.* n.d. Trans. Laura F. Banfield and Harvey C. Mansfield, Jr. Princeton UP, 1988.

Magida, Arthur J. 1996. *Prophet of Rage: A Life of Louis Farrakhan and His Nation.* Basic Books.

Maidens, Melinda, ed. 1981. *Immigration: New Americans, Old Questions.* Facts on File.

Maltitz, Horst von. 1973. *The Evolution of Hitler's Germany.* McGraw-Hill.

Manchester, William. 1992. *A World Lit Only by Fire: The Medieval Mind and the Renaissance: Portrait of an Age.* Little, Brown.

Manning, Aubrey. 1972. *An Introduction to Animal Behaviour.* William Cloves.

Mansfield, Harvey C. 1996. *Machiavelli's Virtue.* U of Chicago P.

Maren, Michael. 1997. *The Road to Hell: The Ravaging Effects of Foreign Aid and International Charity.* Free Press.

Margolis, Maxine L. 1984. *Mothers and Such: Views of American Women and Why They Changed.* U of Calif. P.

Marx, Karl, and Friedrich Engels. 1888. *The Communist Manifesto.* Trans. Samuel Moore. Penguin Books, 1967.

Maslow, Abraham H. 1968. *Toward a Psychology of Being.* 2nd ed. Van Nostrand.

Maxfield, Sylvia. 1990. *Governing Capital: International Finance and Mexican Politics.* Cornell UP.

Menninger, Karl. 1938. *Man Against Himself.* Harcourt Brace.

———. 1942. *Love Against Hate.* Harcourt Brace.

———. 1958. *Theory of Psychoanalytic Technique.* Harper & Row.

———. 1973. *Whatever Became of Sin?* Hawthorn Books.

Michell, H. 1952. *Sparta.* Harvard UP.

Milgram, Stanley. 1974. *Obedience to Authority: An Experimental View.* Harper & Row.

Miller, Richard L. 1986. *Truman: The Rise to Power.* McGraw-Hill.

Montagu, Ashley, ed. 1964. *The Concept of Race.* Macmillan.

Montefiore, C. G., and H. Loewe, eds. 1974. *A Rabbinic Anthology.* Schocken Books.

Morris, William O. 1901. *Napoleon.* G. P. Putnam's.

Morton, Frederic. 1979. *A Nervous Splendor: Vienna 1888/1889.* Little, Brown.

National Commission on Excellence in Education. 1983. *A Nation at Risk: The Imperative for Educational Reform.* USGPO.

National Report on College-Bound Seniors, 1985. 1985. CEEB.

Noe, Ronald, Frans de Waal, and Jan van Hooff. 1980. Types of Dominance in a Chimpanzee Colony. *Folia Primatol.* 34.

Odom, Guy R. 1990. *Mothers, Leadership, and Success.* Polybius Press.

Ornstein, Robert, and Richard F. Thompson. 1984. *The Amazing Brain.* Houghton Mifflin.

Ortega y Gasset, Jose. 1932. *The Revolt of the Masses.* Trans. Anon. W. W. Norton, 1985.

Ouspensky, P. D. 1950. *The Psychology of Man's Possible Evolution.* Alfred A. Knopf, 1971.

Oxford Analytica. 1986. *America In Perspective: Major Trends in the United States Through the 1990s.* Houghton Mifflin.

Plato. n.d. *The Republic of Plato.* Trans. Francis MacDonald Cornford. Oxford UP, 1941.

The Portable Plato. Viking Press, 1948.

Polybius. n.d. *The Rise of the Roman Empire.* Trans. Ian Scott-Kilvert. Penguin Books, 1979.

Rand, Ayn. 1946–1966. *Capitalism: The Unknown Ideal.* New America Library.

———. 1961. *The Virtue of Selfishness: A New Concept of Egoism.* New American Library.

Rhodes, Richard. 1986. *The Making of the Atomic Bomb.* Simon & Schuster.

Riding, Alan. 1985. *Distant Neighbors: A Portrait of the Mexicans.* Alfred A. Knopf.

Riss, David, and Jane Goodall. 1977. The Recent Rise to the Alpha-Rank in a Population of Free-Living Chimpanzees. *Folia Primatol.* 27.

Roberts, Stephen H. 1937. *The House That Hitler Built.* Methuen & Co.

Rogers, Jim. 1994. *Investment Biker: Around the World with Jim Rogers.* Adams.

Ryrie, Charles Caldwell. 1976. *The Ryrie Study Bible: King James Version.* Moody Press.

Safire, William. 1987. *Freedom.* Doubleday.

Sampson, Anthony. 1975. *The Seven Sisters: The Great Oil Companies and the World They Shaped.* Bantam Books.

Santillana, Giorgio de. 1955. *The Crime of Galileo.* Time-Life, 1981.

Schlesinger, Arthur M., Jr. 1986. *The Cycles of American History.* Houghton Mifflin.

Schopenhauer. n.d. *Essays of Schopenhauer.* Trans. Mrs. Rudolf Dircks. Walter Scott, n.d.

———. n.d. *The Philosophy of Schopenhauer.* Carlton House, 1928.

Seagrave, Sterling. 1985. *The Soong Dynasty.* Harper & Row.

———. 1992. *Dragon Lady: The Life and Legend of the Last Empress of China.* Alfred A. Knopf.

Seldes, George, comp. 1985. *The Great Thoughts.* Ballantine Books.

Shoup, Paul S. 1981. *The East European and Soviet Data Handbook: Political, Social, and Developmental Indicators, 1945–1975.* Hoover Inst.

Silber, John. 1989. *Straight Shooting: What's Wrong with America and How to Fix It.* Harper & Row.

Skinner, B. F. 1971. *Beyond Freedom and Dignity.* Bantam Books.

Slansky, Paul. 1989. *The Clothes Have No Emperor: A Chronicle of the American '80s.* Simon & Schuster.

Sluckin, W. 1965. *Imprinting and Early Learning.* Aldine de Gruyter.

Small, Meredith F., ed. 1984. *Female Primates: Studies by Women Primatologists.* Alan R. Liss.

Smith, Huston. 1958. *The Religions of Man.* Harper & Row.

Solzhenitsyn, Alexander. 1963. *One Day in the Life of Ivan Denisovich.* Trans. Ralph Parker. New American Library.

———. 1973. *The Gulag Archipelago 1918-1956: An Experiment in Literary Investigation.* Harper & Row.

Sowell, Thomas. 1983. *The Economics and Politics of Race: An International Perspective.* William Morrow.

————. 1984. *Civil Rights: Rhetoric or Reality?* William Morrow.

Spock, Benjamin. 1974. *Raising Children In A Difficult Time.* W. W. Norton.

Stachura, Peter D. 1975. *Nazi Youth in the Weimar Republic.* Clio Books.

Stanley, Thomas J., and William D. Danko. 1996. *The Millionaire Next Door: The Surprising Secrets of America's Wealthy.* Longstreet Press.

Strong, James. n.d. *The New Strong's Concordance of the Bible: A Popular Edition of the Exhaustive Concordance.* Thomas Nelson, 1985.

Suomi, Stephen. 1974. Social Interactions of Monkeys Reared in a Nuclear Family Environment Versus Monkeys Reared with Mothers and Peers. *Primates.* Dec.

Surway, H. 1955. The Double Relevance of Imprinting to Taxonomy. *Brit. Journ. of Animal Behaviour.* July.

Tawney, R. H. 1926. *Religion and the Rise of Capitalism: A Historical Study.* New American Library.

Taylor, Jared. 1992. *Paved with Good Intentions: The Failure of Race Relations in Contemporary America.* Carroll & Graf.

Teilhard de Chardin, Pierre. n.d. *Writings in Time of War.* Trans. Rene Hague. Harper & Row, 1968.

————. n.d. *Christianity and Evolution.* Harcourt Brace, 1971.

Thorpe, W. H. 1955. The Nature and Significance of Imprinting. *Brit. Journ. of Animal Behavior.* July.

Thorpe and Zangwill. 1961. *Current Problems in Animal Behavior.* Harvard UP.

Time Frame. 11 vols. 1987–1988. Time-Life.

Tinbergen, Niko. 1965. *Animal Behavior.* Time-Life.

Tocqueville, Alexis de. n.d. *Democracy in America.* Trans. George Lawrence. Ed. J. P. Mayer. Harper & Row, 1969.

Toffler, Alvin. 1980. *The Third Wave.* William Morrow.

Toland, John. 1976. *Adolph Hitler.* Doubleday.

Torres, Elias L. 1973. *Twenty Episodes in the Life of Pancho Villa.* Trans. Sheila M. Ohlendorf. Encino Press.

Toynbee, Arnold J. 1947 and 1957. *A Study of History.* Abr. D. C. Somervell. 2 vols. Oxford UP.

Turnbull, William W. 1985. *Student Change, Program Change: Why the SAT Scores Kept Falling.* CEEB.

Tyler, Leona E. 1965. *The Psychology of Human Differences.* Appleton-Century-Crofts.

Understanding Human Behavior: An Illustrated Guide to Successful Human Relationships. 24 vols. 1974. Columbia House.

Urdang, Laurence, ed. 1981. *The Timetables of American History.* Simon & Schuster.

U.S. Dept. of Commerce, Bureau of the Census. 1975. *Historical Statistics of the United States: Colonial Times to 1970.* Bicentennial ed. USGPO.

————. 1984. *Statistical Abstract of the United States 1985.* 105th ed. USGPO.

———. 1985. *Money Income and Poverty Statistics of Families and Persons in the United States: 1984.* USGPO.

———. 1989. *Statistical Abstract of the United States 1989.* 109th ed. USGPO.

Utechin, S. V. 1961. *Everyman's Concise Encyclopaedia of Russia.* E. P. Dutton.

Vernon, Philip E. 1979. *Intelligence: Heredity and Environment.* W. H. Freeman.

Verplanck, W. S. 1955. An Hypothesis on Imprinting. *Brit. Journ. of Animal Behavior.* July.

Verrill, A. Hyatt. 1929. *Great Conquerors of South and Central America.* New York Home Library.

Waal, Frans B. M. de. 1984. *Chimpanzee Politics: Power and Sex Among Apes.* Harper & Row.

Weber, Max. 1904–1905. *The Protestant Ethic and the Spirit of Capitalism.* Trans. Talcott Parsons. George Allen & Unwin, 1930.

Weeks, John R. 1981. *Population: An Introduction to Concepts and Issues.* 2nd ed. Wadsworth.

Wells, H. G. 1920. *The Outline of History.* 2 vols. Doubleday, 1971.

Werner, Oscar H. 1966. *Unmarried Mother in German Literature.* AMS Press.

Wheelwright, Philip. 1959. *Heraclitus.* Princeton UP.

Winterbottom, Marian R. 1953. *The Relation of Childhood Training in Independence to Achievement Motivation.* U of Michigan Ph.D. diss.

Wolf, Josef. 1978. *The Dawn of Man.* Trans. Margot Schierlova. Harry N. Abrams.

The World Almanac and Book of Facts 1975. 1974. Newspaper Enterprise Assn.

The World Almanac and Book of Facts 1985. 1984. Newspaper Enterprise Assn.

The World Almanac and Book of Facts 1995. 1994. Newspaper Enterprise Assn.

Young, Leontine. 1954. *Out of Wedlock.* McGraw-Hill.

Ziegler, Philip. 1969. *The Black Death.* Alan Sutton.

Index